I0136897

John Holmes Agnew

Reply to Professor Tayler Lewis' review of Rev. Henry J. Van Dyke's sermon on Biblical slavery

also, to his other articles on the same subject

John Holmes Agnew

Reply to Professor Tayler Lewis' review of Rev. Henry J. Van Dyke's sermon on Biblical slavery
also, to his other articles on the same subject

ISBN/EAN: 9783744731348

Printed in Europe, USA, Canada, Australia, Japan

Cover: Foto ©Lupo / pixelio.de

More available books at **www.hansebooks.com**

REPLY

TO

PROFESSOR TAYLER LEWIS' REVIEW OF REV. HENRY J. VAN DYKE'S SERMON

ON

BIBLICAL SLAVERY;

ALSO,

TO HIS OTHER ARTICLES ON THE SAME SUBJECT, PUBLISHED IN "THE WORLD."

. BY

J. HOLMES AGNEW.

NEW YORK:
D. APPLETON AND COMPANY,
443 & 445 BROADWAY.
1861.

PRICE:—Single copy, 10 cents; 100 copies, $6; 500 copies, $25.

INTRODUCTION.

THE following pages were prepared for "The World," and written successively as Professor Lewis' articles appeared. His treatise, however, was extended so far beyond a simple answer to Mr. Van Dyke, that, by the time he reached his conclusion, it was thought undesirable, then, to admit this reply into "The World's" columns.

The "American Society for Promoting National Unity" having desired and unanimously recommended the issue in its present form, it is thus given to the public. It will, probably, not reach all the readers of "The World," as was desirable, yet it is intended to give it as wide circulation as possible; and it is hoped that those who have read Professor Lewis' series, will also read the Reply.

It is an independent investigation, the Professor's articles and the Scriptures having been the basis; and all the author asks is an unbiassed judgment on the argument. He thinks himself standing securely on the Bible ground. If not, he has no desire to stand at all.

J. H. A.

April 10*th*, 1861.

ENTERED, according to Act of Congress, in the year 1861, by D. APPLETON & COMPANY, in the Clerk's Office of the District Court for the Southern District of New York.

REPLY.

GOVERNMENT AND OWNERSHIP.

"If ever the moral aspects of the slavery question are to be discussed in its roots," says Professor Lewis, "this would seem a proper time for such discussion. There is a right and a wrong somewhere in this matter, and we think they can be found." My object, in this review, will be to sift the argument of Prof. Lewis, that the chaff, if any, may be blown off, and only the clean wheat of truth remain; to be a pearl-diver, and, if in the shell there be a pearl, put it into the casket of Truth; if only a shell, throw it away. It is best always to grant to an antagonist all that he may fairly claim, all that would strike a candid and unprejudiced mind as fairly his due; and then, on the points, where you have the manifest advantage, ply him with energy. Whatever conclusion is reached, after a fair examination of the question, we mean to accept, without regard to North or South, Republican or Democrat. We know that easy as to cut the air is it, to address readers thoroughly prepossessed with the sentiments you intend to advocate; and hard, on the other hand, as to strike your hand on the edge of a Damascus blade, to utter opinions counter to those cherished by your hearers. We accept the office, however, relying on the good judgment and the patience of our readers, to hear us through. We shall arrive at a conclusion, which, it is thought, will commend itself to the conviction of the Christian church.

In the Professor's initial paragraph, there is too much of the inferential and of the *ad captandum*, too little of the rigid exactitude of naked truth, too high a laudation of the "sublimity of that great, conscientious vote of the North," to which he, doubtless, contributed. It might, with propriety, be asked: Who have been "breaking up the Union, for the sake of" anti-slavery? Who is "giving ease to the consciences of those" who would violate compacts, speak evil of dignities, despise governments, and defy the powers that be? Who is "virtually justifying their proceedings?" The Professor is doing these things quite as manifestly, to many minds, at least, if not to his own, as Mr. Van Dyke, in his sermons, is sustaining the extremists of the South. It may as well, also, be here premised, that Prof. Lewis and myself are, as I have presumed, of one mind in respect to the supreme authority of the Scriptures, as a standard of truth, and that we alike reject the fatal dogma, that human instinct or sentiment, or even conscience, is determinative of moral questions. Men must, indeed, obey conscience, for, if they do not, they do wrong (*relatively*); yet, in obeying conscience, they do not necessarily nor always do right, (*absolutely*) *the right*.

Prof. Lewis first directs attention to a "fallacy to be found in most Northern productions similar to Mr. Van Dyke's," i. e., the adoption of a *via media*, in which the writer avoids the "odiousness of the extremest ground of the extreme South," and yet palliates the Southern idea and action, and antagonizes the Northern. He "distrusts the maxim *in medio veritas*," and says "it is not scriptural." "Truth seldom is precisely in the middle." In reply to this, it may suffice to say that *in medio, midway*, was never intended by the author of the maxim, nor any one else who ever quoted it, to mean that the truth was "*precisely*" in the middle, but somewhere off from the two extremes; as we say of a ship at sea, "she was mid-ocean," not intimating that she was precisely half-way between the two coasts of Europe and America. And then, as to the maxim being "not scriptural," I must beg leave to differ from my learned friend. Not that it occurs *verbatim* in the Scriptures, but that it is of the spirit of the Scriptures, and that the apostles, especially Paul, the learned and the bold, acted it out. When a clearly-defined wrong was done, when an indisputable principle, known and read of all men, was at stake, none was more decided and denunciatory than he; but when it was a question not involving a fixed and immutable principle, though of grave importance, he took the *via media*, the middle ground, and "became all things to all men." His letters abundantly illustrate this, and his reproof of Peter at Antioch confirms it. And what did the college of apostles at Jerusalem, in respect to a question of Gentile rights referred to them? What but walk on the *via media?*

To prove the changes in the line of direction of the *via media*, and the tendency toward the extreme, it is affirmed that "every new move of the stronger extremist has drawn the *mediist* after him;" the direction, because of the corruption of human nature, being downward, from moderatism to extremism. So, then, it follows that the "Republican party," which has, in the Professor's judgment, swallowed up the Abolitionists, as Aaron's serpents did those of the Egyptian magicians, must, after a while, evomit and be itself the eaten instead of the eater; i. e., must, as mediists, succumb to the power of the extremists; or else the dogma of the Professor is not true; or else, if the contrary is the fact in the North, and the mediists have controlled the extremists, and reduced them to "a mere handful, without influence, without votes, and ever growing smaller," then there is no reason why the same may not be true in the South, and the mediists there also (untrammelled, unagitated, undisturbed by the North, and left to work out their own institutions under Providence) finally control and subdue the extremists.

After these preliminaries, and before coming directly to his argument, the Professor concedes that, "as against the Abolitionists, Mr. Van Dyke has borne himself right valiantly," and proved the "anti-biblical and infidel tendency" of their doctrine, because they attack slavery "on the ground of mere natural right." He also "concurs, at least exegetically, in Mr. Van Dyke's view of 1 Tim. vi., and other passages." Now it seems to us clear that, if Mr. Van Dyke's argument is good as against Abolitionists, in Prof. Lewis' judgment, he must mean either that it is good as against raids, personal liberty bills, incitements to insurrection, etc., or as against the Abolitionism which Mr. Van Dyke himself set up and defined as consisting in the " belief that slaveholding is a sin, *is morally wrong.*" "This is its characteristic doctrine and its strength," says the author of the sermon. If the latter, then Mr. Van Dyke's argument is good against Prof. L. and all who sympathize with him in the sentiments of his reply. For, if that reply is an argument for any thing, it is assuredly an argument, or an attempt at one, for the *moral wrong, the sin of slavery.* And, moreover, it is apparent that Mr. Van Dyke is contending, not against an Abolitionism which " attacks slavery on the ground of mere natural right," but against one which maintains the moral wrong, the sin of slavery, on the ground of the Bible and of Christianity. Hence his appeal is to the Bible, in order to meet his antagonists just on their own ground, and to sweep from beneath them the very foundations on which they so triumphantly claim to stand. And precisely here is the essence, the strength, the *virus* of that conscientious conviction of the wrong of slavery which permeates and contaminates the very vitals of a portion of the Northern church. Then, again, the argument of Mr. Van Dyke on the infidel tendency of abolition is good against anti-slavery mediism even, which rejects biblical evidence when it comes in conflict with human instincts, generally adventitious, educated feelings or sensibilities. And to us it seems there is rather a tendency toward this in the reply, if not in the author. The concession made to the soundness of Mr. Van D.'s exegesis of 1 Tim. vi., is immediately qualified by the presumption that the Professor sees " an interior spirit in those texts," " an apostolic stand-point," " a changed condition of the world," which render the exegesis, though absolutely true, " the letter that killeth, instead of the spirit that giveth life." Although cautioned that " it is vain to say that this is a mere transcendental fancy, by which the force of Scripture may be ever turned aside," we cannot avoid the fear that the Professor became involved in a nebular transcendentalism, which, by some powerful reflecting telescope of his own, might be resolved for him into brilliant twinkling stars, and yet leave all ordinary observers the vision of nothing but a well-defined mass standing out boldly and clear to the perception. There is, indeed, "the letter that killeth," and there is, also, "the spirit that giveth" not life, but death; death to truth, death to the Bible, death even to Christ. Now, it is very manifest to every biblical scholar, and such Dr. Lewis confessedly is, that the passage in Tim., treating solely and simply of mutual duties arising from the relations of moral beings, is as wide asunder from any of those cases in which "inspiration itself warns us of danger," of the literal, or letter-interpretation, as heaven from earth. The "letter," the literal meaning here, is just what we want, what we must take. We dare not go beyond it. It is the mutual duties of master and slave, in the plainest possible terms. No fancy, no "spirit," but just what the apostle says. One might imagine that old Origen himself had become transmigrated and embodied in the humanity that would be delving just here for an underlying, invisible "spirit."

We are glad, now, to reach the scriptural argument proper. On the part of Professor Lewis, it lies in the distinction between *lordship and ownership*, or *government and property*, and in the fact that the latter characterizes Southern Slavery, while the former was the peculiarity of the patriarchal and Homeric.

The argument from the O. T. is pronounced "utterly worthless, even as against the Abolitionist," because the slavery which awakens his antagonism is so essentially, so monstrously different from what is called slavery in the O. T., that no fair comparison can be made. Though it should be proven, is the intimation, that slavery existed and was recognized under the patriarchal and Mosaic dispensations, it would be no justification of American slavery. The latter is then portrayed as consisting predominantly in the *idea of property*, and that idea realized in the perpetration of all manner of crimes; in the "crushing out of humanity," "the outcasting from the State," "the reduction of a *person* to a *thing*, a chattel, an animated tool. The former as a servitude, whose predominant *idea* was *government* merely, and that idea realized in exclusion of *caste*, no-sale, kindness, sympathy, familiarity of social life, illustrated by the relation between Abraham and his slave Eliezer. Then is it triumphantly asked : "Have we elevated the idea of servitude?" "Have we been improving it?" "Then may we quote the patriarchs." We have next, consecutively, the following statements and propositions : "both ideas, lordship and ownership, enter into slavery," and "the predominance of the one over the other determines its character." "The *claim* of *power*, even when wrongful, is perfectly consistent with human dignity." Power, the most despotic, is not degrading, though it drive its subject, against his will, to be murdered "at the cannon's mouth," and to leave behind him a lone widow and helpless children in abject poverty. "To be *owned* is degrading." "To be *property*, and nothing more, is dehumanizing, both to owner and owned."

The gist of Dr. Lewis' reply is just here ; and yet, in these statements, and the stirring appeals growing out of them, we seem to find fallacy, unfairness, assumption, and assertion. In eloquent utterings the Professor dwells, at length, on the *degradation*, the *dehumanization*, the every thing that is abhorrent both to Christ and humanity, which are involved in the idea of *ownership*, and *that* the essence, the characteristic of American Slavery. Humanity shrinks from the idea of property in man. Jesus *feels* it, Christianity abhors it, as "brutalizing the race." All this is eloquent, touching, tender. Yet we are here chiefly to reason and to expound ; and the main question is, Are these things so?

Is *ownership* of a fellow-man degrading? Is this a universal idea? Does it belong to the race? History says not ; but the opposite. All ages, all the families of man, have recognized the idea of *ownership* without blushing, have practised on it without the feeling of degradation. And how is it at the South? How, with the man and woman there, accustomed from infancy to the idea, as familiar with it as with that of the parental relation? Do they shrink back appalled at the idea? Have they any such experiences, any such *gefuehl*, as the Germans would say, in connection with this idea, as harrow up the very soul of Dr. Lewis? Verily, no. Then, has Dr. Lewis any right to claim it as an universal idea; any right to enwrap it with his own notions and sentiments, and then insist that, just in that form, it must be realized in every soul? Where, in the history of humanity or in the Word of God, do we find these distinctions so dogmatically insisted on as moral axioms? And how do we know, as he asserts, that the patriarchs never "*sold* a slave?" Because it is not recorded of any one, sooth the Professor. On this principle of interpretation we should allow much not allowed, and disallow much that is allowed. There is a manifest reason why the buyer is spoken of rather than the seller: but, beside this, if one bought, (and this is granted,) another must have sold: nor is it very apparent how an Hebrew could buy an Hebrew, unless an Hebrew *sold* him to him. But see Gen. xxxvii., 28; xvii., 13, 27; Exod. xii., 44; Lev. xxv., 39; Deut. xv., 12. In these and other passages, *selling* of men is distinctly stated or clearly implied. The Professor is also mistaken in asserting that slaves are "never mentioned in the O. T., as property, never reckoned along with the flocks and the herds." See Gen. xii., 15, 16; xx., 14; xxiv., 35; xxvi., 14; xxxii., 5, etc. In all these passages slaves are *reckoned* along with flocks and herds. "Sheep and oxen, and male slaves and female slaves." "Flocks and herds, and silver and gold, and male slaves and female slaves, and camels and asses." "Oxen and asses and flocks, and male slaves and female slaves."

It is clear as day that the *idea of property* did attach to the patriarchal, biblical slavery; to that of Abraham, Isaac, Jacob and Moses. And that it was not the predominant idea, or that the other, *government*, was, is inferentially asserted rather than proved. Moreover, if the idea of property, of ownership was in it at all, as it must have been according to the Professor, being an idea necessary to slavery, then there was not probably at that time, nor is there to be now, ascribed to it that "degradation, that dehumanization, that brutalization," which, in the Professor's mind, are its germ and its casement, its all in all: then the patriarchs and the prophets probably did not feel themselves degraded *by* the relation, nor *in* it.

Why, again, is it necessary to show that "the Texan slave-holder" has "*improved*" the social status of the slave, and advanced him beyond that of the patriarchal, in order to quote the latter in justification of the former? Appeal is made to slavery under the O. T. simply to prove that the *relation* of master and slave existed, was recognized and regulated by law, not that the *same system prevailed*, the same legal or adventitious circumstances accompanied it. And if the idea of *ownership*, or *property* in man is found there, then it is fair to quote O. T. slavery in justification of modern *slavery per se*, although ownership be its basis. Its evils are extraneous, adventitious, growing out of the corrupt passions of man. Its blessings, too, may be great; are great, in very many instances. It were easy to select, in the South, many an Eliezer, many a slave as faithful as Ulysses', and receiving as much of the confidence and respect of his master. We could tell tales of familiar social life there, between master and slave, that would put to the blush the man, who talks loudly of freedom, equality, manhood, lordship, and yet subjects to a deeper degradation the Irish servant, or the *colored freeman*, who does the menial service of the house, under an exclusion from the family-life, from the family board, under a caste of separation and exclusiveness, embittered with wormwood and gall. And does the classic Professor forget what Hector said to his wife, on parting for the war, and *what a slavery* was implied in it, in that early Grecian period, that Homeric age? And sad to say, even the favorite slave of Ulysses, in his absence, had bought and owned a slave himself. We are ready, also, to contend, and to prove, that in the Southern slavery the idea of government" is the predominant one, and not that of ownership or mere property.

And why is "subjection to *power*, however despotic, not degrading," but to be *owned* necessarily so? It is easy, perhaps, to throw a halo of "*glory*" around the idea of power, however dictatorial and tyrannical, and under it the man may march to the cannon's mouth : and yet many a poor creature under the conscription of a despot, torn from wife, children, home, and *driven* to the field of carnage and of death, would gladly forego all "the glory" of the idea, for the quiet comfort of being *owned* and cared for, in health and sickness, in manhood and age. "All that a man hath will he give for his life," even liberty. Yes, life without liberty, is estimated more highly, and that by a divinely-implanted instinct, than the name of liberty with compulsory exposure to death at the cannon's mouth. Nor is this degrading. *Freedom is not the highest happiness, nor the greatest blessing.* I could own a fellow-man, for his good, and neither feel that I was degrading myself, nor him. In this department of the "Reply," there is too much of the "*petitio principii*," too much taken for granted. Besides, slavery is but "subjection to power," even where property is the chief element of the power. It is a power, too, regulated by *law*, which reaches and binds both master and slave. And, though in the abstract, power may not be degrading, yet, in its exercise, it may be monstrously so, both to the potentate and his subject, as in the Emperor Nero. So the abstraction of ownership, the mere relation thus expressed, may be not at all dehumanizing, whilst the exercise of it, the action under it, may be so in the extreme. And, indeed, further on, in his first article, to which we are now confined, the Professor concedes the essence of the argument, when he affirms that, "it is not the mere presence, but the predominance of the idea of property, which gives its chief *moral character* to slavery." If, then, the mere presence of the property-idea, or of ownership, gives no moral character to the relation, property or ownership may exist, and there yet be no bad moral character, *no sin* in it : and if so, then it *may* not be, it *is* not degrading. But strange is it that the Professor should have become so etherealized by his idea of the dignity of power, as to have forgotten the lessons of history, both ancient and modern. All the worst concomitants of modern slavery, which he denounces as the worst the world ever knew, are nothing in comparison with the horrid inflictions of inquisitorial and other powers on their subjects. Even the power of abused capital, and especially of legislation by aristocratic and oligarchic wealth, is incomparably more grinding and debasing to its *abjects*, than the severest lashes ever laid on the back of the poor slave, or the bitterest deprivations and exactions to which he is ever subjected.

And now, as to the charge laid against Southern Christians of an " uneasy conscience," quieted only by the opiate of great blessings to the negro, or by the bitter drug of " throwing the slave from the pale of humanity," and trying to believe him but semi-human, and thus landing in infidelity, it is simply harsh and unfair. It grows, psychologically, out of the transfusion of his own climatic and adventitious feelings into the bosoms of his Southern fellow-christians. He, in like *outward* circumstances, retaining his own interior views, would have an uneasy conscience, therefore, they must. There might, possibly, be more of the " easy conscience " in gliding smoothly along in Northern seas, tideless and stormless ; in walking with the *multitude*, in augmenting the majesty of that " sublime vote," and shouting hosannas with the triumphant, numberless throng! There may, too, be quite a strong " tendency to infidelity " in exalting natural instincts above the Bible, or letting them have free play, without the restraint of revealed truth.

In all this preliminary and foundation-argument, we think our learned friend has erred, in connecting indissolubly with his idea of ownership, all the very worst evils of the slave-system, the flagrant wrongs and barbarities often perpetrated by the godless overseer and the inhuman slave-driver. But the abuse of a thing is no valid argument against its use. The human body is often prostituted and debased by its owner, and even to have one at all may be a degradation in the view of angels, yet none of us would exactly like to be without one, in this life, nor can we, because of its abuse, abate or despise its use, or its propriety.

We think, too, that the Professor has been somewhat carried away by his inwrought feeling about property in man, wrought up to the predominance of sentiment and passion, not in the bad sense, or he would have scanned more closely many of his epithets and phrases. In describing Southern slavery as " the outcasting from the State," it were well for us to remember how utterly an outcast, in this regard, as well as socially, is the *free negro* of the North. In descanting so impassionedly

on " the crushing out of the *human* brotherhood any whose
nature Christ has assumed," it was forgotten that this can have
no logical force, because it applies neither to the immense mass
of Southern Christians who do not entertain, yea revolt at the
idea, nor to those seiolists, who do, for they would deny that
Christ did assume that *semi-homo*, or *homo-animal* nature.
Then, again, when it is said that the slaveholder " if a *ruler*,
in distinction from an *owner*, must be a ruler of brutes, of seeming men, of a half-humanity, brutalized in appearance, though
looking like us," who does not see and feel the extravagance
of the declarations! Why, instead of being brutalized in appearance, the slave, under the slave system, has been lifted
up immensely in his humanity, both spiritually and bodily.
Compare him with his kin, fresh from the bogs or deserts of
Africa; with the cargo of the ship " Wanderer," with the native
Congo or the negro of Guinea!

But our amazement is extreme as we read: " It is said
'Thou shalt not covet thy neighbor's manservant,' and the
text is often quoted to prove the scriptural lawfulness of the
modern human bondage; but so it is also said, 'Thou shalt not
covet thy neighbor's wife.' The argument is as good in the
one case as in the other." That is, if it prove ownership right,
as to slave, so also as to wife. And does it not prove it? Is
it not a manifest recognition, by the Divine Lawgiver, of the
rectitude of the relation, the right of ownership in the master?
If not, how could there be *sin in the coveting?* And if no sin
in coveting, how could it be so emphatically, so positively, for-
bidden? If the neighbor, the holder of the slave, had no *right*
to him, then was there no *wrong* in the *coveting* of him. But
God pronounces it wrong, absolutely forbids it, and thus, by
necessary implication, justifies the relation. We acknowledge,
also, that the argument is just " as good " in the other case
quoted, the coveting of a neighbor's wife. Why not? And
what objection is there to it? None whatever. The prohibition here also proclaims the rectitude of the relation, whether
you call it *ownership* or not, sustained by the husband to the
wife, making the coveting, in this case, just as wrong as in the
other, and no more so. The husband had the right to his wife,

as the master to his slave, and to covet the one or the other was equally wrong. Nor does the fact, that the prohibition is the same in the two cases, prove that *ownership* was the relation in both, at least in the same sense, but it does equally justify both relations, and pronounce coveting in both equally sinful. Neither slave nor wife, each in his own relation, could be coveted, and therefore either could be rightly held. But should it be said that the relation implied in the terms " manservant and maidservant," is not ownership but lordship ; and that the prohibition, therefore, justifies no other than such relation, in any state of slavery, I reply, that this is assertion without proof; and I assert, on the contrary, that the idea of ownership is the idea of the relation here expressed by those terms, and I prove it by appeal to the Professor's own declaration that this idea is necessarily in *slavery*, but more especially by collation of the legal documents and historical writings of the people to whom the Law was given.

And again, if it be said that the prohibition does not imply *right* in the possessor in the thing possessed, but forbids the *coveting* as well where the thing coveted is wrongfully held, our reply is that this notion grows out of confounding *desire* with *coveting*, the latter implying, in any divine enactment, that the thing coveted belongs to another, *is his by right*, moral or legal, or both. Does not *coveting*, also, as a legal term, imply that you would have a right to possess the thing, if not owned by another. In other words, does it not apply only to things lawful, things you might rightly possess, as a *wife*, in distinction from a mistress. This is, perhaps, a new view of the law. We think it the logical and legal interpretation, and would commend it to those capable of judging.

It is not the common idea of the Law, that its language, " whatever is thy neighbor's," implies property in the preceding objects specified, but this, that the *prohibition* itself, the term employed, of necessity implies property and the *right* of holding.

We have extended our argument somewhat on the first article of the Professor, which we think his chief and his strongest ; but we hope not to weary the patience of our readers, in the future discussion. It is a subject of deep interest, and should be well weighed by thinking minds, both North and South. "Too long has the appeal been made to every thing else but truth."

ARGUMENT FROM THE OLD TESTAMENT.

HAVING proved, as we think, the existence and divine re-cognition of slavery under the Old Testament Dispensations, and that property or ownership was a coexistent, if not pre-dominant idea in that slavery, that buying and selling belonged to it; having disrobed the idea of property in man of that garb of degradation with which the Professor had invested it, and exposed his distinctions between ownership and power, as rather fancy than fact; having shown that the ideas and ac-tualities of Jewish slavery were such as to be a proper basis of comparison between that and modern slavery, and having given our interpretation of the Moral Law on this point, it is intended, in this number, to review the Professor's argument on Lev. xxv., 44–46. "Both thy bondmen and bondmaids which thou shalt have, shall be of the heathen that are round about you. Of them may ye buy bondmen and bondmaids. Moreover of the children of strangers that do sojourn among you; of them may ye buy, and of their families that are with you, which they beget in your land, and they shall be your possession. And ye shall take them as an inheritance for your children after you, to inherit them as a possession; they shall be your bondmen forever." This passage proves : 1. Permis-sion to hold *slaves*, not hired servants, for the Professor well knows the distinction between the two Hebrew words ; 2. To *buy* them, and that with money, not ransom ; for this would not apply to the second class, those "begotten in their land ; " 3. To buy of the heathen round about; 4. Of sojourners and their families; 5. They should be *owned*, be property; 6. Be property for life, just that and no less does the word *forever* mean, unless it may indicate that they and their offspring in successive generations *forever*, shall be the possession of the family ; 7. To be bequeathed, in the same relation, as *slaves*, to

2

children. Their "children after them were to inherit them as a *possession*." If the possession of the parents was that of *ownership* obtained by purchase, then was the right and title in the children the same.

It is conceded by Mr. Van Dyke, and the Professor intimates it to be clear, that " what is said of the enslavement of a Jew by a Jew cannot be applied to modern slavery, because, in the former, provision was made for redemption, liberation after a time. This is the universal view, we believe. But is it correct? Why is not the argument as good in its essence, from the law relating to the bondage of Hebrews, as from the passage now under consideration? Although it differs from the modern bondage and from that of Lev. xxv., 44–46, in the provision for a limitation of time and a redemption, there is given a special reason for that limitation, to wit, that the Hebrews themselves had been, as a people, already long in bondage. But beside this, in that very bondage or slavery, there is the same idea of property, of purchase and ownership, as in the other. The time of possession is limited, but the *title*, the *right*, the *relation*, for that time, is the same. It would, therefore, be fair and logical to reason, as well from this as the other slavery of the ' heathen round about,' that the divine law recognized slavery in the relation of ownership, slavery *per se*. Then, if so, that relation in the modern slavery cannot be wrong *per se*."

Without conceding, therefore, to Prof. Lewis or Mr. Van Dyke, what we know is universally conceded, that no argument for modern slavery can be based on the law regulating the bondage of a Jew, let us proceed to examine the Professor's reasoning on the passage quoted above. He denies any force in the argument founded on this passage, in justification of slavery *per se*, and offers two answers. One "greatly weakens" the argument, and the other "renders it utterly worthless." The diluting answer of the Professor consists in the fact, as he represents it, of an utter want of resemblance between the two slaveries, the Jewish and the American. The points of contrast are found in the differences between the two peoples, and in the mercantile feature of the modern slavery; the vendibility of the slave not attaching to the Jewish.

Since truth is our sole object, and fair interpretation or purpose, we feel compelled here to differ with Dr. Lewis, and to dilute somewhat his own argument. When he denominates the Jews an "agricultural, untrafficking theocracy," and the South "commercial, cotton-growing States;" he seems to us utterly to fail in making out a striking contrast. The Hebrews "agricultural;" the Southern States "cotton-growing," i. e., *agricultural*. The Hebrews "untrafficking," Southern States "commercial," the latter attribute scarcely belonging more to the one than to the other; the former not specially characteristic of the Hebrews, their traffic having been, by no means, restricted for those days, as even the biblical history proves. But the burden of the Professor's first answer consists in his denial of vendibility to the Jewish slavery, and his reasoning on the question of God's permission of sin. In order to get rid of the language of the law, "ye may *buy*," and to remove even a "seeming resemblance," he tells us, what he presumes every body knows, that *buying*, in such cases, meant the "payment of ransom," "sometimes the ransom of life." Alas! for the interpretation of our scholarly professor. If the word did mean to *ransom*, in case of captives in war, it did also mean to *buy* with money. What! "*buy* in such cases," i. e., in this case, in this law, means paying a ransom! Let us so translate: "Of them (the heathen) may ye *pay ransom for* bondmen. Moreover, of the children of strangers that do *sojourn* among you, and of their families, which they beget in your land, for them ye may *pay ransom.*" No reference here to captives *ransomed* from death by substituting a life-slavery. Evidently simple trade, traffic. Children born in the land, too, could be *bought* into perpetual slavery, transmissible to posterity. Does *buy*, in this case, mean to pay ransom? What ransom, and for what?

Having thus attempted to remove all possibility of comparison between the Jewish and Southern slavery as founded on this Levitical law, by denying the usage of language, and astounding both the common sense and the learning of his readers, he reverts to the old idea, argued at length in his first

2

article, that although " permitted to buy, there is not a word
of *selling*," " no reckoning of them as property with corn, wine,
herds, flocks." The false assumption on both these points, has
already been fully met by quotations from the Scriptures, and
need not be repeated. The Professor might well be here called
on for proof of his oft-repeated assertions, when he so fre-
quently demands evidence of Mr. Van D.'s statements. That
there is too much of mere vendibility attached to the slave by
many in the South, might be conceded, and yet that this idea
did not attach to the Hebrew's slave, and that it was never
abused by the wicked, our author has utterly failed to prove.
The Professor should know that there was a *slave-mart* among
the Jews. Yet, we are obliged to discover that, even in this argument on the absence of the mercantile in the Jewish slavery, its
presence is inadvertently confessed. " There are intimations in
the Jewish history that it was, at certain times, more mercenary. Then we hear the thunderings of the prophets, as in Isa.
lviii., 7, ' Loose ye wicked bonds, unbind the servile knots, set
free the oppressed, *break asunder every yoke.*' " If, at times,
more mercenary, then, at all times, positively mercenary. This
is precisely as we contend and prove. And, moreover, we
think the " *then* thunderings of the prophets," when *more*
mercenary, leaves us clearly to infer that the mere mercenary
idea itself was not an object of the prophet's denunciation, unless the Professor will here retract his own affirmation, and fall
back on the extremest literal interpretation, making the thunderings apply to the relation itself, to simple slavery *per se*.
But it is not possible for him here to accept the *literal* interpretation. He would not stake his scholarship on it; for just
here, in prophetic, excited denunciations, is the place for figu-
rative expressions, for the " spirit, the interior view."

But now the Professor is obliged to meet a sharp question
of some objector, to wit: " Is it consistent that God should
give a permission, and then rebuke men so sweepingly for taking the benefit of it?" and his reply is: " God does permit
what he rebukes men for doing. He permitted Balaam to go
to Balak, and then sharply rebuked him for going." But to
reconcile the discord in this passage, we are told that " God

gave him permission to go that he might *bless*, but Balaam went to *curse*, and so God rebuked him, because he went to *curse.*" The case does not prove his proposition that God permits what, *just what*, he rebukes men for doing. He permitted the *going*, rebuked the *cursing.* The "unreasoning beast" might here arise, if there were for him a resurrection, and pronounce, in the presence of our learned Professor, his own words: "'God is wiser than men,' says Mr. Van Dyke, where he would rebuke the Abolitionists. We have no thought at all of disputing the truth of that proposition, but might think it capable of some application to others, who assume so boldly to be the exclusive defenders of Deity."

But the permission given in the passage of Lev. xxv., which, according to the Professor, was to *pay ransom* for captives, we are further taught, was a merciful permission, growing out of the "spirit of the times." The *spirit of the times* justifying God in permitting, in allowing and regulating, by statutory enactment, slavery *per se ;* the buying of men and women into bondage to be a possession and an inheritance forever! If this was sin in itself in the sight of God, we see not how God could thus enact, maugre the argument on Balaam and the ass. We think as little of the assertions about "slave hunts in Moab," and "Solomon's never thinking of bringing home, from Ophir, human chattels along with his gold dust, asses, and ivory." *Perhaps* he needed none just then : *perhaps* he was not accustomed to go just in that direction for such articles, whilst that was the place for the traffic in gold dust, asses, and ivory."

We confess to a dulness of perception which does not see the force nor propriety of the argument on the fugitive slave law of Deut. xxiii., 15, 16. The newly adopted view of the Professor applies it equally to all slaves, whether of Hebrew or of foreign origin, whilst generally it is limited, in construction, to the latter. Our objection to the Professor's interpretation lies chiefly in the fact, that it seems a necessity of scholarship and of the usage of language, to interpret the pronouns, *thou,* *thee*, in this case, as generic, not specific, as meaning the nation as a body politic, a people and thus including each individual. Consequently it is in contrast with the "heathen around about," and has no application to an Hebrew slave. This view is confirmed by the *usus loquendi* of the entire chapter and of almost the entire book, and indisputably by the 16th verse itself. " He shall dwell with *thee*, among *you*, (the people,) in the place of his choice, in *one of thy gates. Thou* shalt not oppress him." In one of *thy* gates, cannot mean a gate of a particular man or family, but a locality in one of the tribes. Besides, the rendering is utterly inconsistent with principles of legal construction. No clause of a general statute can be so rendered as to mar the consistency of the whole. And there would be a most manifest inconsistency in the enactment of authority to buy slaves of the heathen, with a perfect license to the slave to escape from his Hebrew master and an absolute prohibition of his surrender. Believe it, who can! Not I. It is a contempt on Deity.

The Professor is lame, also, here in his " strict construction" of the lawyers, when he says that, " had the words *escaped unto thee from his master*, meant *from the heathen*," the language would have been general and collective ; " who shall have escaped from any *of the nations round about thee*." Now, we humbly think not, because whilst the usage of speech, and the very law itself necessarily point to the foreign fugitive, the equally necessary implication is, that he had a *master* there, not that he was an *immigrant* from Moab or Idumea. Consequently the law would specify that fact, and exonerate the Jew from whatever right or claim there might be in the *heathen* master.

The Professor winds up this first answer to the argument founded on Levit. xxv., by the insinuation that " the permitted bondage " was " a statute not good," Ezek. xx., 25—" for the Israelites," and that the liberation of a slave was regarded by " the early Christian church as a good work." In reply to the former, it is only needful to read Ezek. xx., especially vs. 10, 11, 33, *seq.*, to satisfy one's self that the " statute not good " had no sort of reference to the slave-code, but that, on the contrary, it was one of those described in vs. 10, 11, as good and now disobeyed, although special reference is had to idolatry and Sabbath-breaking. In regard to the latter, it is *ab extra*, it belongs not to the point at issue. If the proof were adduced, it could be fully met. We shall here and now simply assert, that, in the " early Christian church," during the first three centuries, the liberation of a *slave*, in itself considered, was not pronounced a " good work," the liberation of *captives* from the chains of barbarians was ; nor was the *idea* of property in man discarded as abhorrent, but the right even of a wicked, heathen master was recognized, and on the baptism of his slave, the obedience of the latter to the former was rigidly enjoined, whilst the testimony of the Christian master to the obedience and good behavior of his slave was requisite to his admission to baptism.

The second answer of Dr. Lewis to the reasoning and conclusion based on this passage of Leviticus, is this, that under the Christian dispensation there has ceased to be any " heathen round about," that the word was " the antithesis of Jew, not of Christian." Consequently, if no heathen now, authority given the Jews to buy slaves of the *heathen*, cannot be plead in justification of any slavery under the present dispensation. This reply, he thinks, " utterly sweeps away this stronghold of the pro-slavery cause," and he calls on any one to detect a fallacy in it. With due deference to the Professor's reasoning power, which, however, we think a little diluted with water-colors, we shall assail the argument very briefly.

The Jewish was a " nation kept apart," " a people by itself," " the type of the better humanity to come." " Hence a Jew was nearer to a Jew than to any other race." " He was allowed to hold bondmen from the heathen." " Who are heathen now ? is the vital question." " The wall of partition has been broken down." " In Christ all are one—all free— free spiritually, free from all that degrades, free from ownership." " As, anciently, Israelite to Israelite, so, in the ' new covenant' with humanity, is every man to every man." " All are brethren now." In all this, there is a deep truth, but a shading thrown upon it, which makes it look like a different thing from the reality. It might be replied to two of the above statements, that as " Jew was more to Jew than to any other race," so is American to American ; and as the nation

was a "type of the better humanity," and possessed slavery,
that might also exist under the antitype, the higher humanity.
But the general reply to the general and pervading tenor of
the above quotations, is, that they much mistake the precise
idea of the relation between the Jew and the heathen in the
passages referred to, and of that between the church and the
world of the present day. The wall of partition between Jew
and Gentile was indeed broken down in Christ. But was it,
at all, in the sense indicated by Prof. Lewis' comments? If
the Apostle meant, by this, any thing more than that Christ,
by his life and death, broke up that dispensation which had
limited the blessings of the true religion to one people, and
excluded the Gentile world, and secured the future dispensation
of the gospel to the latter as well as the former, to all, then it
seems to us he failed to make his meaning clear. In Christ
Jesus all are indeed one; all are, indeed, free. But how?
Does this signify that the whole Gentile world has become
Christian, is possessed of the blessings which are proffered to
faith in Christ? Or does it simply mean that there is no longer
a "peculiar people," "to whom pertaineth the adoption, and
the glory, and the covenants, and the service of God, and the
promises?" Can it, does it mean, that what Jew was to Jew
anciently, joint participant in peculiar privileges in fact, every
man is now to every man, joint partaker of his proffered mer-
cy? Are all, indeed, one in Christ, or only they who are one
in him by faith? Are all "spiritually free," in any sense other
than this, that all peoples are alike entitled to the blessings of
the new covenant? Certainly not in the sense of being in
Christ by faith; assuredly not in the sense of Christ's own
declaration: "if the Son shall make you free, then shall ye be
free indeed." And can the Professor show us, in the bond or
in the "spirit" of it, that Christ's freedom includes, as he says,
freedom from ownership or bondage? And when he descants
eloquently on the "dogma of the life or blood unity of the race"
as kindred to that of the incarnation, does he mean to say that
the dogma is peculiar to the new covenant? Does not that
very dogma find its basis in the very first chapter of the Bible,
and run equally through every page of the Old as of the

New Testament? But aside from all this general reasoning or interpretation, do we not " detect a fallacy " in the very statement of his main proposition : " The Jew was allowed to hold bondmen from the heathen " ? To warrant his reasoning and justify his conclusion, it should have inserted the little word *only* after " *heathen*." For in answering his vital question : " who are the heathen ? " he comes to the deduction that now there are *no* heathen, in the *then* sense of the word, and hence the conclusion, that there can be no authority from that law for human bondage. Thus is " utterly swept away this stronghold." But since the premise fails to be true, the conclusion falls with it. The logic is thus : Ye shall buy of the heathen. There are now no heathen. Therefore, you cannot now buy at all. But suppose we put the case truthfully thus : Ye may buy of your *brethren*, also, for a limited time. Africans are your brethren. Therefore ye may buy of them limitedly. All we mean to say here is that *ownership* is equally recognized in both species of slavery, that of heathen and of brethren, and therefore, should the Professor even be successful in sweeping away the stronghold, by his denial of the applicability of that law, because of the present non-existence of any heathen correspondent to those designated in the statute, the argument from the Mosaic statutes would not fail. Appeal could still be successfully made to the law allowing the slavery of a brother Jew, in the *relation of ownership*, and thus justifying what, in the Professor's view, is the distinctive and damning characteristic of the modern slavery. For if ownership could exist, under certain circumstances, for seven years, it could under others, for life. And if, for a few years not degrading, then not at all.

But we find another fallacy, in the statement, that " Israel was the type of the better humanity." Is it not rather the type of " the spiritual Israel," " the body of Christ," his church universal ? Or rather is it any type at all, in the proper sense of the word ? Read more from the Professor : " Of your fellow-men ye shall not make slaves. Ye may *rule* them, sternly, if necessary, but ye may not *own* them." " This is a sin *per se*." " The church is for all nations. We have all one home, one brotherhood, as well as one Saviour." All this is well, properly understood : but our metaphysics does not permit us to see what more relation it has to the question of slavery, even *ownership*, than to an hundred other things. If this glorious truth of the unity of the race in Christ, the breaking down of the wall of partition, the oneness of the home, of the brotherhood, of the Saviour for all nations, is to be thus plead against human bondage; in the same spirit and with the same propriety, may it be plead against all social wrongs, against all distinctions, and launch us on the dark sea of socialism. These things, these biblical expressions, are not to be thus interpreted. No law of interpretation will justify it.

And yet again, what biblical exposition follows. "Ye cannot plead any more the language of the old law: 'they shall be your *possession*, to make bondmen of the nations round about you. God has given them to Christ—' the heathen for a *possession*.'" Right on the basis of this, there follows a warm appeal to the Christian world to go out and take possession of the nations, in the name of Christ, *just where they are*, to which we add a hearty Amen. Yet, this seems to us very little, and certainly not directly, to the point: and the idea attached to Christ's *possession* of the heathen is amazingly new and strange. It is this: God has given the heathen, i. e., all the Gentile world, to Christ for a *possession*, therefore no man can *possess* or own another in the relation of slavery. The possession of Christ is now substituted for the possession under the Levitical law. Can it be possible that the Professor has overlooked the fact that he uses the word possession in two different senses? It cannot be that he so interprets that prophetic gift of the heathen to Christ as to mean any thing more, any thing else than that they shall all finally come to the knowledge of Him as the Redeemer, shall be imbued with the spirit of his gospel and become members of his kingdom of righteousness, peace, and joy in the Holy Ghost. Any other interpretation, and especially such as the Professor intimates, would lead to monstrosities in hermeneutics. But then, such possession, such as was manifestly contemplated by the Spirit and the prophet, lies entirely outside of the question of human bondage, utterly beyond all the merely governmental and social relations of life. It rather regards and permeates them all, " rendering to Cæsar the things that are Cæsar's," but not rudely laying its hand on the established order of governments. A man may be a slave and yet be the possession of Jesus in the very highest sense preconceived by the prophet; and even in the clanking chains of ownership, and by means of it, have tens of thousands become the freemen, the possession of Christ, the one ownership not interfering with the other, yea, co-existing with it. And it may not be anticipating to say, just here, that these very Gentiles, these " sons of Adam, brethren redeemed by Christ," were the slaves of the times of Christ and his Apostles. And assuredly all that is so glowingly said about telling " the African that Christ has *bought him*," has no direct application to the subject in hand; nor all the rhetoric about telling him the story of the cross, where he is; nor · that about " climatic nationalities : " for the poor manacled slave of the South, " just where he is," can as well be taught that Christ has *bought him*, as the degraded, brutalized humanity " on the banks of his native Chadda and Zambesi ; " and as to climatic temperaments and local habitations, there is as much reason for the immigration of the African to our Southern clime, as the Saxon and Celt to our Northern.

The third article of the Professor, now under consideration, closes with some " home questions ; " all of them, perhaps, not in the best taste, and each and every one easily answered. The substance of all is contained in the following : " When a slave in the South becomes a Christian, will he be still a *heathen*, subject to enslavement, or will he be entitled to his freedom ? " Let Paul to Philemon answer this. He having done it, we abstain. Yet we may answer the question, by asking another : Did the Jew free his heathen bondman, if he became a Jew ? That is an all-sufficient reply. Yet we might further ask : Was it not the great object to make him a Jew, and redeem him from the idolatry of heathendom ? Should the Professor take the alternative that the slave could not become a Jew, so as to enjoy religious privileges, then he would most triumphantly upset his whole argument, by the confession that this Hebrew slavery surpassed, in caste and cruelty, the worst form of the Southern.

ARGUMENT FROM THE NEW TESTAMENT.

PRELIMINARY to the argument derived from the New Testament, Professor Lewis reverts to his two *constituent* ideas of slavery, power and property, which he pronounces logically distinct. Intending to be brief, it needs only to be remarked, that, if property is one of the *constituent* ideas in slavery, one without which it cannot be, or *stand together*, then it follows that it was in the idea of slavery, patriarchal, Jewish, Roman, or Christian, as well as American; and consequently his long argument on the property-idea, the sum and substance of his entire argument, is by himself essentially annihilated. As to their being logically distinct, thus much may be said : Property necessarily implies power, but power not necessarily property. · He talks, also, of the "morality of slavery" as determined by the "absence or presence, predominance or subordinance" of the one or the other idea: so that morality is attributable of slavery, if only power be present, although he had before said, it will be remembered, that it did not depend on the *mere presence*. "Property," too, it is contended, "is essentially · *selfish*, power essentially *unselfish*," a proposition which needs more than assertion, for thoughtful minds, one which it would be difficult to maintain, for few things are more selfish than power and the desire of power, ambition. The application of the statement to the Southern planter is very unfair and untenable, because, even assuming the truth of his proposition, he must allow that the slave there is held not only as property but as person also, as *chattel-personal*.

The Professor now grants that we cannot judge of individuals, whether in this or that one the selfish or unselfish idea predominate, but we can form a correct judgment of a national slavery, a slavery of an age. "The individual can tell for himself whether he is a *man-owner* or a *man-ruler*," that is, according to the logical distinction of the Professor, whether he is selfish or unselfish, whether he *governs* only for good, or owns only for evil. Now it seems to us very clear that a Christian master can be both *owner* and *ruler*, and yet be as unselfish in the relation, as most men are in the other relations of life; and it is equally clear that one may be an *owner* and own for the good of the slave, *unselfishly;* another may be a mere *ruler* and not an owner, and rule tyrannically, *selfishly*. Now, in the former case, when the master holds, *under law*, "unselfishly or for the good of the slave," is he justified in holding, in *owning?* The Professor's reasoning affirms that he is, and thus he surrenders himself captive to his own logic.

The case of the centurion is just here adduced as a case in point, an apt illustration of the *idea of power*, the ruling or governing for good, and to this is injected a doubt whether the *ho pais* of the centurion was a slave. It is an extreme case that takes advantage of every doubt, and to the man in danger of execution our laws freely accord it. The Professor will at least allow that the probabilities are strongly in favor of the judgment that he was a slave, not only because he is called *doulos* as well as *pais*, but because we should scarcely expect a Roman centurion to hold his servant in any other relation : and if so, *ownership* in the centurion was not inconsistent with unusual piety and faith in Jesus, "such faith as he had not found, no, not in Israel." But the case is even stronger. Can the Professor believe that, posited as the Saviour was with him, he could or should have abstained from pronouncing on the inhumanity and unchristianness of *property in man*, if he regarded that, as the Professor does, the most " degrading, dehumanizing of ideas," and especially in view of the relation of humanity to this very Christ, so graphically portrayed by the pen of this ready writer ? If that was a sin, particularly if a crying sin, could Jesus, the immaculate, any more have withheld from putting this disciple to the test on that point, than he did from trying the amiable young man by demanding of him the sacrifice of his property? Never! never! This were far more degrading to our Master than *ownership* of man to man. The thought of such a possibility, we confess, detracts at once from that high, pure, ethereal, superhuman, divine conception we have, and love to hold, of Jesus. When we feel ourselves obliged to abandon that idea of him, we shall feel like accepting him only as a great Teacher, suited to his day. Which may it never be!

Ah, this holy and blessed Master of ours looked more to the inner than to the outer life, more to the existence in the soul of a living faith in himself as the Christ, than to the social and governmental relations of the man, if so be, in those relations, he evinced the spirit and temper of the Christian. This man was an officer of the Roman empire, having soldiers under him and slaves subject to his will, faithfully discharging political and social duties, whilst he permeated them all with the spirit of Christ. We hear of no release of his soldiers, no emancipation of his slaves, but we do read of his loving the one and exacting obedience of the other.

The author next distributes the slavery ages into Patriarchal, Jewish, Roman, Christian, applying to each his *property-scale*, and attributing to the last the *maximum* of the property-idea. Its essence is "gain *per se.*" The Roman was "less mercenary," had "less *caste*," though "more cruel, less dehumanizing," "hurt humanity less." Now the whole of this reasoning, if it may be so called, is simply the expanding of the idea of *ownership*, which the Professor has labored, first to evolve as the *summum malum*, the radical dehumanization of the race, the substratum of all that is evil in slavery, and then to attach preëminently to the American Slavery. Hence his declaration that Roman lawyers ever pronounced slavery as against natural right, but never made a Dred Scott decision. Now, the former it would be difficult for him to prove, the latter has no application, for at Rome there were no such constitutional provisions as with us, never an occasion on which such a decision or the opposite could possibly have been demanded.

But granting, argues the Professor, that the Roman slavery was worse than the modern, as most would certainly concede, yet the silence of Christ and his Apostles as to its evils, their exhortations to patience and submission and cheerful obedience on the part of the slave, constitute no justification of slavery. But we beg leave here to differ. The silence of Christ and his Apostles, their never having, on any occasion, whilst so many offered, uttered one word of condemnation, even in letters to the churches, in which they recognize its existence, is most amazing and inexplicable, if they deemed of it as the Professor does ; if the mere *status* were so monstrously degrading and dehumanizing.

And again, however much exhortations to submission may fall short of justification of the thing submitted to, in themselves considered, yet we think the gist of the argument, as we should put it, has been wholly overlooked by the Professor. Beside the fact that the exhortations embrace cheerful, hearty *obedience* to a rightful authority, as well as submission to hard and cruel impositions by the froward, it is apparent that, if the thing itself, the mere ownership or holding of the slave in bondage under the Roman law, were wrong, as idolatry, murder, theft, cruelty, etc., Christ would have denounced that, as well as its abuse. But further, the strength of argument, in our estimation, lies rather in an unnoticed direction. See 1 Cor. vi., 9, 10 ; Gal. v., 19–21 ; Eph. v., 3–5 ; Col. iii., 5–9 ; 1 Tim. i., 9, 10 ; 1 Pet. iv., 3, 14 ; Rev. xxi., 8 ; xxii., 15. In these several passages, "the works of the flesh," and the sins which indicate an unrenewed nature, exclude from the city of God, and subject to "the second death," are specifically and reiteratedly recited, and yet, not in one single instance is slavery enumerated or most distantly hinted at. And it might be pardonable here to make use of the *argumentum ad hominem* and remind Dr. Lewis, that, as the non-enumeration of slaves, in which we have shown him to be mistaken, however, with other property of the Hebrews, as flocks and herds, is to his mind proof positive that the property idea was wanting in the Jewish servitude, equally conclusive must be the absence of slavery from the inventory of unchristian and damning sins. The damning and unchristian idea must not attach to it, cannot belong to it. Remarkable indeed it is, that this crying sin of ownership in man is never once denounced nor even hinted at as a crime which must blot one's name out of the book of life, though it be held, by many of Christ's followers, to be a sin of scarlet dye, and "a covenant with hell."

It is appropriate here, also, to recall the fact that, whenever

the unity of the Christian church is spoken of, the oneness in
Christ, it is in such wise as to recognize this relation, and include the bond and free : " for by one spirit are we all baptized
into one body, whether Jews or Gentiles, whether bond or free,
for the body is not one member, but many." " There is neither
Jew nor Greek, there is neither bond nor free, there is neither
male nor female : for ye are all one in Christ Jesus." " Where
there is neither Greek nor Jew, circumcision nor uncircumci-
sion, barbarian, Scythian, bond nor free : but Christ is all and
in all."   Col. iii. 11.   In the exhortations based on this verse,
exhortations to the elect of God, to wives, husbands, children, fathers, servants, masters, the chief relations of life, in
which, on the one part, obedience and submission are duties,
hear how this clear-headed, heavenly-instructed apostle, just in
this connection, just on this fundamental statement of the
union of all classes, bond and free, in Christ, hear how he talks
to the *bond:* " Servants," slaves, " obey in all things your masters according to the flesh ; " your *owning* masters.   " And
whatever ye do, do heartily, for ye serve," in thus doing, " the
Lord Christ."   Now, if these passages prove or assert any
thing, they assert this : that in the brotherhood, the body of
Christ, there do just as certainly exist the master and slave,
as the male and female, the Jew and the Greek, and that the
one Spirit, permeating the one Body, shall alike sanctify them
all, not disrupting, but combining these relations with the
" bond of perfectness."

We now come to the Professor's comments on 1 Tim. vi.,
1–5, and we confess to not a little surprise, in view of the in-
tegrity of our brother.   His running commentary first perverts
the evident meaning of the passage, and then finds the " key
which unlocks the whole difficulty right here ; " " a believing
master never could regard his *believing douloi,*" slaves, " as
property."   " It is Christianly inconceivable ; " " he could not
*own ; " " the golden rule would not allow it ; " " the loving
thoughts of the apostle could not entertain it."   The perver-
sion lies in the insertion of the word " *believing* " before masters.   These servants, he says, " are enjoined to obey their
masters, their *believing* masters."   " Persons who teach other-

wise are condemned." Now, if any one, scholar or no scholar, will turn to the passage and read vs. 1, 2, he must see that, in the first, there is not only no *believing* there, but that the specification of the second necessarily excludes the qualifying term *believing*, from the first. In the first verse it is: "Let as many servants (all) as are under the yoke, count their masters, etc." In the second: "And *they that have believing* masters, let them not despise, etc." Out of as many as are under the yoke, out of the entire class of slaves, some have *believing* masters. These are singled out in the second verse, and thus become specific, and the duty here enjoined varies a little from that in the first verse, and is founded on a specific and different reason from the honor required of all, in the first. Whether the Professor is teaching "otherwise" than conformably to the apostle's injunction, it were well for him to search out, lest his own description of such teachers attach to himself, and he be found "doting about questions of words, and perverse disputings" *logomachies* "of men destitute of *the truth*."

"The key, also, which unlocks the whole difficulty," has, somehow, become so rusty since it left the Professor's hand, or so involved in transcendental and instinctive ligaments, that it will not work in the wards of the lock. It fails to open the safe for us. It is "mere moonshine" to try to get over the plain, simple truth of this and other similar passages, in which the same obedience is taught to the master, who was "froward," *unrighteous*, and "buffeted his slave for doing well," inflicting suffering "wrongfully," *unrighteously;* mere vain *logomachy*, to endeavor to blunt the edge of the truth, by rhetorically enlarging on the "apostle's loving thoughts," "the Christian inconceivableness, the impossibility of a Christian master regarding his slave as property," the abnegation of "ownership," "the oneness in Christ," etc., etc.

Who told our author that these things are so? Has God? Has Christ? Have the apostles? Has any thing higher than his own instincts, his own psychological condition? We presumed, at the outset, that we agreed as to the sole standard of truth, but we begin to fear. We affirm and prove that the early Pauline Christian master *could own, and did own*, under law, as in the South, and did not, nor was required to, emancipate. Where, as the Professor so often asks, where the requirement?

Nor does it seem to us that the Professor gains any thing for his cause, by his contrast between the political status of the Roman empire and the American republic, there being, in the former, none of "those social rights and social duties so much boasted of in the latter." Because, forsooth, there was "no citizenship, in the modern sense, no voting, no political rights," therefore the slave must submit and be obedient, under the tyrannical *power ;* but here, where there is citizenship, let him seek it, let him have it! But there was a citizenship under the Roman power. Paul had it. There was the freeman and the freedman, there was position enough higher than that of a slave. Why not urged to seek that, as well as now, the higher political freedom? And we doubt, besides, whether the Professor advocates the universal right of voting by all men, of all colors.

And now again, our author affirms that the "real issue" is, that there is not a word of buying or selling slaves in the N. T., nor a case of discipline for the sin anywhere recorded. Most marvellous! "Not a word of buying and selling." "Not a recorded case of discipline for it." It would be strange, indeed, if the apostles should stop, in their letters, to tell us whether Epenetus, Andronicus, Apelles, Aristobulus, Rufus, Gaius, Erastus the chamberlain of the city, ever bought or sold a slave. These transfers of property in man were probably common in those days and not noteworthy, the Professor's psychologic idiosyncrasy to the contrary notwithstanding, although even he thinks it "barely possible there might have been something with the *resemblance* of a sale, but which was merely a method taken by one brother for placing another brother in a better condition"!!!

And then, as to "discipline," why should there be any? The presumption is the other way, that there would be none, if neither Christ nor his apostles denounced the relation as wrong, and especially if recognized as a customary and legal act. But further, where are the recorded cases of discipline for covetousness, for calumny, for slander, etc., etc.?

It may be well enough for the Professorial chair to dilate on clerical blindness, and to express astonishment " at this *pretended* argument from the New Testament, which amounts to nothing, even when put in the strongest light." It is barely possible that they who think they. see, see not, and become " blind leaders of the blind." At any rate, we think the Professor particularly unfortunate in the quotations he makes to offset this strong light, and make it seem to be darkness. " If a man smite thee on the one cheek, turn to him the other," quotes the Professor : and triumphantly asks, thereupon : " Does that justify the smiter and the smiting ? " Most assuredly not, is our reply ; but there is, in this case, no legal nor recognized relation of any kind, governmental or other, between the smiter and the smitten, none, whatever, but the universal relation of man to man as brothers of the Adamic family. " Honor the king." " Does that prove monarchy ? " Why, no ; but it does prove the right of the reigning power to the honor, and the duty of the subject to render it. It here proves a relation, and an instituted relation, out of which grow rights and duties. And only when the investiture of authority is monstrously abused can the rights and duties cease. So of the other quotations. Those I have given are the strongest.

And now our author closes up his argument by a linguical, critical disquisition on the word *doulos.* " It may denote," he says, " the servile condition. It may signify a *subject.*" The Professor has not read Aristotle, Plato, Xenophon, the tragic and comic writers of Greece to so little purpose, as not to know that *doulos does* mean, and preëminently mean, a slave, man in a servile condition, whilst it *does* also signify a subject. And that it does signify *a slave* in the N. T., in those passages on which our argument mainly rests, he assuredly cannot candidly and critically deny. But " there is a word in the Greek language," proceeds the Professor, " that is always servile, ever used to denote slaves as *property,* the word *andrapodon.*" It is true that this term has a very servile smell about it, and one does not like to handle it much. For this reason, perhaps, the Doctor so quickly dropped it. Had he handled it a little more, turning it over and over, he probably would have found some of the properties he attributed to it suddenly evanishing : *e. g.* : " exceedingly common in the classic Greek," " very familiar wherever Paul travelled," " always used with the servile notion," " denoting that that to which it is applied is a *thing* or chattel, without true personality." It need not be so wondered at that the New Testament and Paul never used it, although " so common in Athenian Greek." The reasons, doubtless, were, *first*, that *doulos* was the usual word to express the *slave relation* of the Roman empire, and that *andrapodon*, instead of being " exceedingly common," " very familiar wherever Paul travelled," etc., was exceedingly rare, nor did it, as asserted, " denote a *thing* without personality," but a *person sold* into slavery ; *secondly*, that Paul and other apostles would naturally prefer, in full recognition, however, of their servile state, to employ a term not *so* degrading as *andrapodon*. Why should he choose to denominate these Christian slaves, *vile things*, fit only to be *at the feet* of another, as the word means, or to be " kicked and cuffed." There is no conceivable reason why Paul should, notwithstanding his recognition of the right of property in the master, ever make use of a word, uncommon at the time, and specifically designed to lower the humanity-idea. Nor does the Professor, in our view, establish his scholarship by his criticism on the word *andrapodistes*, which he translates, *slave-trader ;* in our version, *man-stealer.* 1 Tim. i. 9, 10. " The law is made for patricides and matricides, for man-slayers, for *men-stealers*, etc." The " association " here, in which the apostle puts the *andrapodistes*, is such, he thinks, that Paul could never have applied the idea of human property, the thing in which the *andrapodistes* dealt, to a man, much less to a Christian brother. The association is truly bad enough, but it is most unfortunate for the Professor that the *master*, the *slaveowner* merely, is not one of the members of the association. It is only the " *slave-trader*," or *man-stealer*, according to our version. And we verily believe, with Herodotus, Plato, Xenophon, and all good lexicographers, that the *slave-trader*, in the apostle's category, was first the stealer, and then the *seller or trader :* he did the former in order to the latter. The only representatives of the class in our country are those who kidnap other people's slaves, and abet those who do, by building underground railroads and writing books on the inhumanity and horridity of slavery : for the word distinctively means *one who kidnaps, steals free men or other people's slaves for the purpose of selling.* Moreover, as in the South the *slave-trader* is despicable, and not admitted into society, whilst the *slave-owner* has a high social status, so the same distinction was probably made in the apostle's day. The one was a legalized and reputable social relation, whilst the other excluded the perpetrator from the pale of a high civilization. Hence the apostles associated the slave *stealer and trader* with the " unholy and profane, murderers of fathers and mothers, perjurers, etc.," whilst he left out the slave *owner* or master. Easy it is for the learned Professor, from his own stand-point, to seize on certain passages of the glorious gospel of the blessed God, and, with the aid of imagination, infuse into them his own idiosyncracy ; but whether his stand-point is biblical, is quite another question. Since 1776 it has been *supremely easy* in this land of peculiar liberty, to portray in glowing colors the beautiful form of freedom, to represent lovely crowds sweetly kissing her feet, and other multitudes throwing their festal wreaths over her head and neck, whilst they make the very heavens to ring with their plaudit hosannas. But instead of all this, to go and sit down as a worshipper at the pedestal of naked, angular Truth, where probably few will sympathize with your veneration, is not so genial. Yet is it a higher worship than the other.

And now, just now, it is very easy, and it may be very popular, to talk beautifully of some of the spiritual ideas of the Gospel ; yet this may all be quite incidental and transcendental to the argument. It may be palatable, indeed, to serve up a dish of highly spiced sophistry, and pass it round among the guests for something solid ; but it will turn to wormwood in the mouth and to gall in the stomach. Such we deem those closing passages of the Professor. They are solely applicable to the purely *gain-loving* master, to the abominable abuses of slavery, whilst the biblical argument relates only to the thing itself, to the relation of master and slave, constituting mutual rights and duties.

One thing is very certain, that, if apostles sent letters to churches, they must have intended them to be understood as referring to things then existing, however applicable, also, to things future. And no Greek, nor Jew, nor Roman of that day, could possibly have put any other interpretation on the words of Paul and Peter than this: that obedience on the part of subordinates was one of the first and highest of Christian duties; that subordination was ordained of God; that the relation of master and slave was consistent with Christianity, though it were a relation of ownership, and that mutual rights and duties grew out of this relation, incumbent on both; that to be a Christian slave of even a " froward " master was not a matter to be " cared for," and might be a privilege, whilst to be a Christian slave of a " believing " or Christian master, was to be in one of the most tender and loving relations of life; and that he who taught otherwise was " proud, knowing nothing " of the subject, and not to be accepted as a Christian teacher. " From such withdraw thyself," says the apostle. So that, really, whilst Northern ministers and churches, in refusing fellowship with slaveholders act without authority, and contrary to the teaching and action of the apostles, Southern churches and ministers might quote Scripture, if so disposed, for non-intercourse with such Abolition teachers, and exclude them, on the authority of Paul, from recognition as ministers of the truth.

And now let us look a little more closely into the " interior spirit " of the Gospel on which the Professor descants so largely and so warmly. We confess, here, to seeing differently from the Doctor. Our spiritual eye may be affected with a cataract or a paralysis of the nerve, unfitting us for reading the Word intelligently; and yet, we are much inclined to believe, rather, that the Professor has borrowed some spiritualistic glasses of modern days, which have the power of throwing a mist of obscurity over the printed page of the Gospel, whilst they reveal, in large letters, some otherwise invisible lines. Or he reads, perhaps, some Palimpsest copies, in which the original writings, long defaced, are illumed with the interior view, not perceptible in the common version.

To our vision this seems the inner meaning and spirit of the whole Bible, the " apostolic stand-point " as well ; to wit: that the material is for the moral, the mutable for the immutable. The whole creation travaileth in pain together, waiting for a redemption. Earth crumbles, elements melt, the heavens are rolled together as a scroll. Life is a vapor, a shadow, a passing cloud, a weaver's shuttle. Its relations are of little account. The fashion, the shapes, the forms, the relations, the all of this world, is passing away. Look beyond. That is Christ's doctrine, as well as of Moses, prophets, and apostles. There even the tenderest relation of life ceases, and they " neither marry nor are given in marriage." It was of little moment to the sweet singer of Israel, whether he were the king on the throne or the subject at its foot, whether the son of Jesse tending his father's flocks on the hill-sides of Judea, or the crowned and jewelled monarch on the summit of Zion. In this view, also, Christ, the executive of all government and the head of a kingdom not of this world, thought it not worth the while to stoop to the consideration of the mere temporary relations of earth, not touching the established and existing forms of social and political life, not even inquiring whether a man were master or slave, except as to the mutual duties of both, but ever looking beyond and pointing to higher and eternal relations, to be secured by faith and obedience, in every condition and position of life. He regarded submission to Cæsar, even to Nero, thus illustrating the *higher life*, as of far more importance to the subject than the rupture of the bonds of organized society.

Let us not, then, think so much of hurling thunderbolts at the head of the Southern master, of building " underground railroads " to run off the slave, of sending emissaries, living and lifeless, to hurry them up to a false sense of their rights, of breaking their chains, and unbinding their bonds, of giving them *political* liberty, as if this were the acmé of earth's hopes and blessings. Let us not think that to be " born of Abraham," is the excellence of life, but let us rather hear the teaching of Jesus, when he says: " If the son shall make you free, then shall ye be free indeed." Yes, there is something higher, better than mere human freedom, better than descent from the free and the noble, something that permeates the soul, and makes up an interior life, which is comparatively regardless of outward circumstances and temporal relations; something that lifts a Lazarus above his pampered lord, that inspires songs in the prison, whose music drowns the clanking of chains and breaks the dungeon doors; a something that welcomes faggots and bonds of slavery, if it be but the Master's will; something which lights up a smile of joy on the beaming face of the Christian slave never reflected from the brow of the ungodly and froward master, which makes him happier in his toils, though under the lash, than if merely crowned with all the freedom which earth and state could give him; something, in fine, which should lead us all to sing, not, " Give me liberty or give me death," but give me Christ or give me naught. A freedman in him, it matters little whether I be the subject of a tyrannical monarch or the citizen of a free republic; whether I toil, from childhood up, in the dark, miasmatic mines, or in the close, oily, fibrous atmosphere of the ever-clinking factory, or in the kitchen cabinet of a master, or the cotton-field of the planter. I would rather be a slave all my days, and sit at the feet of Jesus to learn patience, humility, and meekness, and then go to wear the laurels of victory in his heavenly kingdom *forever*, than to possess here the highest honors freedom can bestow, and then sink, a lost soul, into the darkness of eternal night. I do not say that to be all this and be qualified for it in freedom is not, in some wise, better; but I do mean to say that prophets, and Christ, and apostles, thought liberty of little account; in the comparison, scarce worth a thought or a word.

See the apostolic earnestness: " I determined to know nothing else, save Jesus Christ and him crucified." Ah yes, may the Professor say, as a ground of pardon and of reconciliation. True, but I take a higher point of observation, a standpoint from which is seen all that the other presents, and bright and beauteous visions beyond. *"Know nothing else."* Yes, all the gorgeousness of earth's trappings is just nothing; all the mere adventitious surroundings of man are mere bubbles: to be in Christ is all, is every thing. Whether a man be a slave or a freeman, whether a capitalist or a laborer, whether a serf or a lord, whether a subject or a sovereign, is to me of no consideration. To think of these things, to dwell on man's *rights*, and woman's rights, as the all-absorbing aim and effort, is just as if, whilst I could direct my glass to the burning glories of the Sun of Righteousness and to the pearly gates and golden streets and ethereal mansions of the heavenly city, I should turn it rather to the floating specks or the dark spots in that sun's atmosphere and the dreary abysses of the second death. Never thus did Paul, nor Peter. They deemed it better for the slave even to continue in his social status, and there to exhibit the transforming power of the gospel, than to grasp after liberty.

And if Jesus thought it not needful for him to reprove the pious centurion for holding office under a most tyrannical power, and at the same time holding property in man; (and that he did no scholar should dispute if He thought it well to receive this man to intimate fellowship); and to commend his faith to the pious of all ages; if He deemed it not degrading nor dehumanizing to *own* a fellow man, why should we shrink from the contamination of contact with slaveholders? why should we, in the spirit of the feeling, "Stand off, for I am holier than thou," denounce and curse him, and put caste upon him in both church and state? Oh, for more of Christ's humility and self-abasement. "He thought it not robbery to be equal with God, yet took upon him the form of a *servant*." It were better for us to follow his steps, take his guidance, do as he did in this matter, than to be foremost in advocacy of human rights and universal liberty, maugre all the jewels it might set in our brow. Let Him be our teacher, and to whatsoever that teaching shall lead, let us gladly follow.

I cannot believe that Jesus Christ ever intended that his church should make aggressive attacks on governments or on organized legal relations in state-life or social-life. Government was his own ordinance, and to violate it a greater sin and evil than to antagonize its institutions as to the relations of social and political life. " My kingdom is not of this world." It permeates all governments, all kingdoms, all dominions, all states. Intended to be adapted to the Oriental, the Indian, the Islander, the African, the all of peoples and of governmental forms : not to disturb but to control ; not so much to guard " Natural Rights," as to give new rights and to infuse a spirit of life into all and over all.

Now, there is a ground on which North and South, freeholder and slaveholder can meet, Lewis and Palmer, Hodge and Thornwell, N. Adams and N. Rice, Barnes and Ross, a panoplied host, clad in the armor of the gospel, the shield of faith, the helmet of salvation, and the sword of the Spirit. Thus accoutred and thus led, our legions shall go forth, conquering and to conquer, and, instead of fighting shadows and abstractions, beating the air, shall fight the good fight of faith, and under the banner of the cross, which ever waved over the apostles' heads, shall deal deadly blows to the enemies of our faith : and, under the great Captain of our salvation, shall enter the citadel and subject the Prince of the power of the air, even Satan, the Deceiver of the nations and the enemy of all righteousness.

SLAVERY AND THE CHURCH.

In this article, Prof. Lewis begins by laying down some conceded principles, the chief of which is, that " the power of the clergy to affect the world for good or ill, can have no second place."

But the Professor finds in the clergy and in the church little recognition of this controlling power, but " a wide desire to find some easier or less responsible place," a disposition " to talk of Christianity as a power smoothly mixing with the world, moulding it by the silent efficacy of doctrines never preached, of a spirit never exhibited, insensibly leavening it without any disturbing force." Men, who adopt extreme views, requiring a wresting of the Scriptures for their support, are very prone to become harsh in their judgments and extremists in their charges. The clergy, undoubtedly, under a deep sense of their weakness, amid the dark and damning powers of sin and Satan in this accursed world, often cry out, "Who is sufficient for these things?" and feel deeply and humbly that they are but "earthen vessels;" yet it is too much for the recluse Professor to charge on the ministry of Jesus Christ *in this land*, the absolute desertion of their "high calling," the dastardly choice of expecting powerful effects from "doctrines never preached," "a spirit never exercised;" the "desire to find some easier way" than aggression on the world, the world "spiritually," as he says; *i. e.*, the world in its sinful principles and ungodly practices. *Tantum sufficit.* We fear, more and more, the power over the Professor of the *one idea of ownership*.

We now come to the great question of his fifth article: "Has the church moulded politics, or politics the church?" and the Professor answers it thus: "The Christianity of the South, the Christianity, to a wide extent, of the North, has been moulded, and continues to be moulded, by the politicians." "The clergy have followed in the worldly wake."

With beautiful, christian "sarcasm," too, with an irony, for which he apologizes, by calling it "the irony of fact," he pours out a torrent of bitterness on those of the clergy who might assume that the change of view on the subject of slavery was attributable to the influence of the church, growing out of a more independent biblical study.

And now, to the proof of his own answer to the question, to wit, *that politics has controlled the church.* What is that proof? Wherein does it consist? *First*, in the fact of a mere "whisper, and hardly that, in condemnation of the Dred Scott decision." Io! triomphe! to Dr. Cheever! And, "why have our churches," the Prof. asks, "felt so little that deep wound to Christianity, as well as to humanity?" This is at best a negative proof, though in reality failing in every attribute of evidence. To be proven: *Politics control the clergy.* Proof first: "The clergy have failed to condemn and denounce the *Dred Scott decision.* Now, in our humble opinion, there is no relation in the proof to the proposition, and of course no rea-

soning, no logic. It takes for granted what is not true, that
the clergy is appointed to review the decisions of the Judicial
Powers of the Government, and if it fail so to do, it is under
the control of politics. Whereas Christ, the Master and Head
of the clergy, emphatically declined, in more than one case, to
undertake any such review, or to give any judicial decisions,
saying : "My kingdom is not of this world." "Give unto
Cæsar," leave unto Cæsar, "the things that are Cæsar's."
"Who made me a judge?" And if there were any force in
such a reason, it were just as forceful to adduce the mere
whisper, and hardly that, in condemnation " of the clearly un-
constitutional " Personal Liberty Bills.

Moreover, it is quite as Christian and quite as facile, to presume that the abstinence from " condemnation," in this case, on
the part of the ministry, grew out of a higher conception of
their calling than that implied in the Professor's charges ; a
conception resting on both the precepts and example of the
Master, and of the great Apostle to the Gentiles, and leading
them to regard the preaching of Christ and Him crucified as
of far more import, obligation, and utility, than to be revising
and denouncing the decisions of Supreme Judges, presumed to
be acting under the solemnity of their oaths. The " Dred
Scott decision " was simply a legal, judicial interpretation of
the Constitution, which the Court was sworn to interpret, by
constitutional law, and which it sustained, also, by a process
of reasoning founded on facts and their relations, which meets
the general approbation of unbiassed judges and of thinking
men. The pulpit, certainly, could not, with much propriety,
or authority, from the Master, undertake to denounce it as unchristian, antichristian, wicked, or of " the world." And even
though a Boanerges, or an Iconoclast, here and there, should,
in a frenzy, deem himself officially appointed to thunder in the
political heavens, and thus to crush the idols of the political
church ; and though a quiet monk, or son of consolation even,
should shout after him, *All hail!* it would not follow that
they two only were the faithful ministers of Christ, the sole
interpreters of his Gospel, the purest specimens of vicegerency

on earth. Nay verily; but rather they, who preach "the truth as it is *in Jesus*," and walk humbly with God.

In regard to the decision itself, a single word. The Professor pronounces it, a "sinking of the colored man to the level of the brute," a "deciding that he is no *member* of the state, that is, *no member of humanity ;* " and he quotes Aristotle in confirmation : "Out of the state," says the greatest philosopher of antiquity, "man ceases to be properly man ; " cut off from "all *membership* with a social human organism, he sinks to the level of the brute." The Professor knows, as he must have read the philosopher, that this author includes the slave in "the social human organism," in municipal society, in the state, and of course, as it seems to us, had no reference whatever to a slave, as ceasing, in that relation, to be "properly man," and sinking to "the level of the brute." He evidently refers to man in a state of barbaric individualism, being, in no sense, part or parcel of a regulated community, a state. His rendering, too, of the Dred Scott decision is *sui generis.* It decides, he says, that the slave is "no *member* of the state at all, that is, no member of humanity." Now, first, his statement of the decision is untrue, and secondly, his expletive still more so. It does not follow that, if the decision were that he is no member of *the state*, he is therefore *no member of humanity ;* and it is gross injustice so to represent either to himself or to unthinking readers. Nor is it true that the decision pronounces the colored man "*no member* of the state." Only that, under the Constitution, he is not entitled to the *rights of citizenship.* The Professor sees the difference between this and his statement.

His second proof of the assertion, that *politics control the clergy and the church*, is no more negative, but positive. It consists in taking a stand-point of his own, and there summoning up before him, on the one hand, the General Assembly of the Presbyterian Church of these United States ; on the other, the celebrated Southern statesman, John C. Calhoun. Now, the former of these august personages in the spectacle, stands up mighty and majestic, holding in his hand the act of 1818, a very Lutheric bill of denunciation against slavery. But, having thus bombasted awhile, with tremendous gesticulation and ejaculation, this awful personage quietly subsides, and, in a dissolving view, gradually evanishes into nonentity. The latter, appearing as "a young politician," then as "a member of the Senate," and then "Vice-president of the United States," and then, in the foreground of the picture, "the champion of slavery," "the oracle, the Bible of the Southern States;" and though with "no great power of individual statesmanship"(? !) though "a disappointed, worldly politician, with no rank as a Christian, even if a nominal believer," (who made thee a judge?) yet driving off his antagonist, the General Assembly, chasing the dissolving view into a dim shadow, and himself filling the foreground, background and middle, the all, of the canvas.

In other words, and without a figure, the Professor quotes the action of the assembly as the noblest Abolition testimony, represents it as lying a dead letter on the old minutes, essentially, though not formally repealed ; whilst the rise and the disappointment of Calhoun in his unmet aspirations for the Presidency, became marked by his announcement of a new doctrine of slavery, which led the clergy to a new study of the Bible, resulting in a general adoption of his views in the South, and extensively in the North. This, then, is the Professor's second and chief argument, to which he devotes two whole columns of the "World."

Forty-two years ago, the General Assembly denounced slavery as an awful sin, equalling "the Abolitionists in strength of language." About forty-two years ago, John C. Calhoun just "rose into notice as a young politician." The politician and the ecclesiastical act were born together, the one, like Minerva, full sized and equipped ; the other an infant stripling. But, lo ! as we gazed, the mighty man evanished, the stripling became a power in the country. Therefore, says the Professor, the stripling conquered the giant. Calhoun was the *cause* of the failure of *the act*. *Politics controlled the church.* Calhoun beat the drum, and the Christian forces assembled. He gave the word, the panoplied hosts fought under his banner. The Great Master's voice they could no longer hear, nor any more fight under the banner of the cross. Poor deserters; we pity you! Why do you not now, since your leader is gone, a disappointed politician, without a particle of piety, too, why do you not, we beseech you, hear the trumpet call of the valiant Professor, and, under his lead, retrace your steps, and, by a counter-march, wheel into the legions of the great captain, accoutred in all the armor of the Abolition-regiment?

A few passing comments. The Professor attributes the new study of the Bible by God's ministers and people, to the dictation of Calhoun. Is it not possible to see a better motive? —"Politics," he says, "has moulded our biblical and theological thinking." Why is this singularly true of one class of ministers? Why not as easy and as true, to say of the Professor and his sympathizers, that their "biblical thinking is moulded by politics;" that mighty Northern politicians and their doctrines of "non-extension" and "irrepressible conflict" control him?

And when he intimates that the "learned and devout English, Scotch, and German commentators do not discover the doctrine," of biblical slavery, that it is found only "in association with slavery," what does he mean? I aver that all of them, who are recognized authorities in hermeneutics, including also our own, do interpret the Bible words, and phrases, and passages, bearing on the subject, in such way as truthful exegesis requires, and as sustains the positions disputed by the Professor.

We wonder that, as the Professor has changed his own views, and turned a complete *sommersault* in *five years*, which he has *nobly* acknowledged, writing himself, "Lewis *versus* Lewis," a rare humility; we wonder he could not conceive that the Presbyterian church, or many in it, might vary their views of The Act, in *forty-two years*. He, at least, should have made some allowance for his brethren, rather than berate his own church as he does. Perhaps beating up recruits, and trying to frighten learned divines and unlearned laity into his ranks! It is very manifest, at least, from the tenor of his closing remarks or exhortations, in which he calls on his church, to "go back to her old testimony," to "repeal, renounce, repent," or

" enforce in word and discipline," with " the decision of a power having the keys, that an assault is intended, perhaps in the next assembly. And then, to " *re-examine Scripture* instead of holding fast to an *ecclesiastical action*," is the " casting down of Zion." An *ecclesiastical act* above and beyond *Scriptural study* and doctrines based on it, what shall we say of it? Rather too high!

There is, throughout this article, we are sorry to see it, and to say it, an undue, and unfitting censoriousness, sarcasm, and obloquy of God's ministry and church—an essential Abolitionism hard in its terms.

SLAVERY AND POLITICS.

In his sixth article, the Professor continues the proof of his proposition, *that politics control the church, and slavery politics.* Facts, he says, prove it. And the first fact is, that the nation's existence is imperilled, and slavery is the cause. This " fearful element of evil in our nation's infancy was suffered to remain," in expectation that " the spirit of freedom " would soon extinguish it. " Without this pervading sentiment, the Constitution would never have been formed." This is, indeed, one view of the case, but whether the *fact-view*, or not, is another question. There is a different view, quite as clearly, at least, yea, more clearly written on the page of history, that *without slavery*, the Constitution could never have been formed; and, perhaps, further reading might convince us that it was not " held everywhere and by all, that the spirit of freedom would soon cause to disappear every thing not in perfect harmony with it;" indeed, that there was far from being an expectation by the fathers, that slavery would die out, " by letting it alone." Instead of the epitaph on our country's tomb being, " *Died of slavery*," it were well for him who writes it, to search deeply into causes, and scrutinize carefully on the post-mortem examination, in order to see whether the truthful inscription should not be, *Died of unchristian meddling with slavery, and consequent violation of compacts.* Whilst it was " let alone," for nearly fifty years, it grew side by side with the freedom of the

North, the one symbolized by the sturdy oak, the other by the tall and graceful palmetto. But when the spirit of Abolitionism began to work and to leaven the masses of the North, it could not be exorcised ; but, possessing its subjects with a furor, it made them meddlers in other people's matters, and they spread an infecting virus even into the body politic, which marred its beauty, maimed its limbs, and shore it of its auburn locks.

So a nest of spiteful vipers might lie in repose in the cradle of a sleeping babe, or coil harmless around its limbs, until roused by some demon spell ; and then, and not till then, would they infuse their venom into its blood, and eat out its life. The poisonous fangs were, indeed, in this case, the immediate cause of death, yet those fangs lay still in their sheath, never spit out their venom, nor affected the beauteous thing, until irritated from without by some tormenting goad.

We look further, and through the article, for the other *facts* "barely to state which is to render the conclusion incontrovertible ;" the conclusion that slavery and politics control religion ; but we can find *none*. There is the expression of an evident feeling of *goneness*, as the doctors might say, while the Professor descants on the fading away of the "hope that our Christianity would heal it," the "indifferency to which good men have given their clerical countenance," instead of preaching against this *political* evil, as he himself here sets it forth ; which, by the way, did not the apostles. The *goneness* becomes an *apoplexy*, when, in conclusion, he again dilates on that awful "Dred Scott decision," and almost pronounces judgment on Mr. O'Conor, the Tract Society, and all men and ministers who cannot, and do not, see in it the very virus of the damned, and denounce it most lustily from the consecrate pulpit of the church. There are good men and true, North, South, East, and West ; there are holy messengers of the cross, who read and interpret that same judicial decision very differently from the Professor, and many, too, who may read it much as he does, and yet not deem it of their special duties, as he does of his, to thunder against it from the pulpit, nor to write it down through the Press.

The great difficulty with our Professor here, as elsewhere, is, that, with wizard wand he conjures up unreal witches, and then, as easily, with wizard wand, bids them down again into their wonted darkness.   He is evidently undertaking to establish his theory that *ownership* for gain is the essence, the all in all of slavery, and that this is utterly inconsistent with the practice of the golden rule.   And, whilst he evidently expects his opponents to include in the idea of slavery, all and every of its concomitant though unnecessary and unusual abuses, he himself refuses to accept the real issue, to wit : not whether slavery abounds in abuses, but whether a slavery legalized and regulated by law, consisting essentially in a right to the time, talents, and services of others without their consent, with a right to sell the same, and a correspondent obligation of care, kindness, protection, and provision, on the part of the *owner*, whether such a slavery is inconsistent with the principles of the Bible, and the practice of Christianity.   It is likewise overlooked that the slave is always called a *person* to distinguish him from other property.

When, also, he denies the application of the golden rule to the system of slavery, and asserts that servile ownership cannot exist under it, he becomes involved in one of his transcendental clouds, and cannot see the bold principles of the Bible standing out like great promontories in a sea of light and love. The exposition of this golden rule, given by its great Author himself, is this : " Thou shalt love thy neighbor as thyself." Such is his summary of the second table of the Law, as it is called, embracing our duties to our neighbors ; and the golden rule covers the same ground, not that of duties owing to God. Now, the last of the laws of the second table, the tenth commandment, as well as the fourth, clearly recognizes the relations of slavery, property-slavery, too ; and Christ, therefore, embraces it in his summary or law of love, and thus proclaims its application to " a servile ownership," equally with all the other relations recognized in this commandment.

Again, if this " claim of servile ownership," this slavery, which we are discussing, " lies out of the pale of Christianity," and cannot consist with the golden rule, it is amazingly strange that the Author of the rule, after having promulgated it and laid it down as a principle to be put into the corner-stone of his church, should nevertheless forget to remind the centurion that his "servile ownership," his masterly relation to his *doulos*, (for it is *ho pais* only in Matthew, and that, too, means slave,) his *slave*, "lies out of the pale of Christianity, out of the kingdom of God, in a region of outer darkness," so utterly inconsistent with his fundamental law, that it "could have no place under it," and must be abandoned.

And again, Paul and Peter must have understood the significance of that golden rule of the master, quite as well as any teachers of modern days, and they, in their injunctions on masters and slaves, never even hint that servile ownership was outside the law of love; but, on the contrary, by application of its principle to the mutual duties of such relation, positively place the *relation itself*, not outside of, but inside, and under this heavenly and Christian Rule.

THE BLOOD-UNITY OF THE RACE.

IN his next chapter, the Professor with a great deal of the "inner sense," the sentimental heart, and an almost utter negation of the pure intellect, although he again quotes Aristotle, the "Pure Intellect" philosopher of antiquity, proceeds to comment, both dramatically and sentimentally, on the text of Paul on Mars' Hill : "God hath made of one blood all nations to dwell upon all the face of the earth." "Its application to slavery was obvious enough," he says; but Paul's higher object was not "to preach merely a political jubilee," but to lead the soul to that all-embracing article, that all men are the "offspring of God," and that "He hath made of *one* blood," of one life, "all nations." And then he asks, with rhetoric interrogation, "Can one such being *own* another?" It might be queried whether Dr. Lewis is justified here, in charging Paul with preaching a "*political* jubilee," but we let that pass.

The Professor, as if haunted by his new evolution of the idea of *ownership*, runs off again into a prolix eulogy of his distinction between *ruling* and *owning*, or *government* and

4

property, just as if it ever needed a new bolstering up, like a very feeble, sinking patient. This, it seems to us very much to need, and we leave it to its fall without adding another blow.

Having transfused, as he presumes, his own degraded notion of owning into the feelings of his readers, he leaves it there to work its effect on the conscience, strengthening the idea, meanwhile, by superadding that " the blood is the life, the one generic life," which flows alike in all, and binds each member to every other in a relation of *kinship*, which must forever forbid the idea of ownership of a fellow-man, a *kinsman*. Yet the Professor did, in an earlier article, most strenuously contend that Christ had bought us, *owned* us, that we were *his possession*, and that hence no one else could *own* any of us, any of the race. The interpretation we did not accept; but we may ask the Professor whether ownership is in Christ degrading, such ownership as he there assigned *to him?*

He now ascends higher than the one generic life, the one *blood* of the first Adam, and confers on the race " a divine humanity," even that derived from Christ's assumption of it, his new sinless humanity coming out of the old ; and thus, historically and generically connected with it, elevating the whole, both antecedent and subsequent, to his own human life. " Christ makes a new bond, a new generic, or life-bond, between all the sons of Adam."

But this is not all. " There is a higher relation still," a divine life growing up on faith in Jesus, but still finding its " ground " in the universal renewed human life imparted by the incarnation. Having thus built up three humanities, the first Adamic, the second Adamic, and the divine, or that of the Christian brotherhood, the Professor reiterates his old question with a triple emphasis : " Can two such sons of God stand in the relation of *owner and owned?* " Why, although the Professor " feels that this is not a mere *mystic sentimentality*," we yet cannot avoid asking, *Did any two such sons of God ever stand in such relation?* And, *has Christ, the Head of all this triple humanity, the embodiment of it, if we may so say, has He ever told us that they cannot stand in such relation?* To the latter we are bound to reply, *nowhere*. To the former, that Christ and his apostles have led us unhesitatingly to believe that many did, in their day ; and, in our own, we think we have seen them. But we find, in the Professor, instinctive sentiments for Christian principles, personal idiosyncrasy for biblical facts. Yet, to ward off the " charge of sentimentalism," he advises us that this " argument is the same in substance as was made, two thousand years ago, by one who was called the ' Pure Intellect,' the unemotional reason." He refers to Aristotle's treatise on *philia, friendship,* in his Nichomachean Ethics, Ch. 8, Bk. XI. " There can be no true *philia,* no real human friendship," says this unemotional philosopher, according to Professor Lewis, " between a *despotes,* as owner, (the Professor's translation,) and a *doulos,* as property, or a thing owned." Thanks are due our scholar for these translations of *despotes and doulos, owning master and owned thing or property,* the very same we are wont to make of these terms in the New Testament, and which, we are sorry, the Professor forgot, when he translated there, and hope he will evermore remember, both when he reads for himself, and interprets for others not learned in the Greek. Notice, also, the use of *doulos,* not *andrapodon,* by the old sage, just when he calls the slave *property.*

The reason Aristotle gives for his denial of philia between the *despotes and doulos, master and slave,* is this : " where there is no *koinon,* there is no *dikaion,* and where no *dikaion,* no *philia.*" " As a *slave,* therefore, there can be to him no friendship," " in other words," adds the Professor, " no human relation," which Aristotle does not say, although much in the practice of saying just what he meant. Indeed, he allows the opposite, that there can be a human relation, although no friendship. It is further declared, also, by our Professor, that " the apostle could never have regarded the relation as one of property," or he could not have enjoined the duty of obedience. The idea is that there could be no such thing as *duty* in such condition, no " *community,*" no " *right,*" no *mutuality* of any kind, no *relation.*

To all these presumptions, as to what apostles could do, or

could not do, we have only to say: *that is not the question*, but
what they did do, and the necessary inferences from their act-
ual doings. As to Aristotle's doctrine, that *friendship* could
not exist between master and slave, his definition, embracing
the requisites for it, renders his conclusion a necessity. It is
very true that toward a mere *thing owned*, toward the slave in
that sense, there could not be *philia;* yet toward him as a
man, as having moral qualities and an emotional nature, though
in the servile condition, there could be, and Aristotle knew
there was, *philia*, friendship, and more than friendship. And
so did apostles think. All their instructions imply that, whilst
the master legally *owned* his slave, he yet could, and should,
regard him as an object *beloved* for the Great Master's sake.

Thus far had we written without consulting Aristotle, relying on his pure intellect for the belief that we had given his
real views. But on going to the Astor Library, (our own being boxed for removal,) and renewing our acquaintance with
the old philosopher and metaphysician, we were gratified to find
the case even stronger than had been supposed ; but we confess to a little surprise, on finding that, as in translating
1 Tim. vi., 1, the Professor had added a word neither in the
original nor in the version, so here he had unfortunately
omitted *just that part* of the very passage quoted from Aristotle, which is *absolutely essential* to its fair understanding, to
the expression of the real view of the great philosopher. We
quote him in full : "There is no friendship (*philia*) toward, or
in relation to a slave, wherein or in as far as he is a slave,
(*doulos*,) for there is no community, (*koinon*,) joint participation.
In as far then as he is a slave, there is no friendship toward
him, but (how important to the sense of the sentence !) in
as far as he is a man, *human*, (*anthrōpos*,) there is also certainly friendship to the extent of his humanity, (*kath hoson
anthrōpos ;*) for there seems to be a sort of 'mutuality of
right' (*dikaion*) with every man toward or in relation to every
one capable of community (*koinōnēsai*) in law and compact."
He had said before : "In as far as, or to the extent to which,
there is joint participation, community, so far, to that extent, is

there friendship, for there is also the right, justice, (*dikaion*,) 'mutuality of right.' "

From this passage it is luminously clear that Aristotle's idea was totally different from that of the Professor, and just as manifest that his idea was misapprehended and misrepresented. Aristotle had laid down *to koinon* as the basis of friendship, the essential to *dikaion*, right or justice. Equality was not essential to it, whilst *humanity*, community of nature, was. Hence a monarch could have a *philia* friendship for his subject, a father for his child. A common nature, humanity was here, although equality was not. Hence no *philia* toward an animal, though *philēsis*, *fondness*, there could be. None toward a thing without life, animal life, *apsuchos :* none, for example, between the artisan and his tool. None toward a slave, (*doulos*,) in as far as he is a slave, for a slave, *as such*, is an animate instrument ; the instrument an inanimate slave. Yet regarded as a *man*, having a *koinon* with his master in humanity, there could be for the slave a *philia*. All this makes it evident how Aristotle viewed the slave as a *chattel-personal*, an instrument of his master for use, service, and yet jointly partaking with him of a humanity which brought him within the domain of the *philia*, or friendship.

It is worthy of note, too, in passing, that Aristotle, in this same chapter, represents tyranny as the deflection from monarchy, the bad form of that species of government, yet government still. But " in tyranny," he says, " there is no *philia*, friendship, or very little, nor justice, (*dikaion*,) nor *koinon*, community." This, remember, is the so much lauded *government, lordship*, as distinguished from slavery, *ownership*, and yet in it there is *no philia*, the very negation which makes the Professor's hair stand on end, when he thinks of it as not belonging to the relation of slavery ! And Aristotle says yet more on this subject, right here. " In Persia the authority of the father is tyrannical, for he uses his sons as slaves. So is the authority of the *despotes*, the master. This, the latter, however, is *right ;* that, the former, wrong, owing to the power of different circumstances." A tyrannical exercise of authority by a *master* justifiable, *right*, *dikaion*, says Aristotle, but not by a father.

To show that this greatest of ancient philosophers did not hold the view attributed to him by the Professor, and impressed on his readers by the manner of his quotation, I take the liberty, here, of quoting somewhat from his Politics, Bk. I.—" Society is not a mass, but a system, implying distinction of parts, with many moral and physical differences, relative and reciprocal, the powers of one supplying the deficiencies of another." " To form a commonwealth from elements of equal value and dignity is absurd." " Forecast should guide improvidence, reason subject passion, and wisdom command folly." " Only those are *inalienable* rights, which one cannot exercise for another." " What persons are presumed to have and yet cannot exercise, it is folly to call inalienable." " A perfect or complete family consists of slaves and free." " The parts of a family are master and slaves, husband and wife, parents and children." " By *law* one is a slave and another free; but by nature there is no difference." " A slave is relative to use, the possession and property of his master." " Slavery is founded both on utility and *justice*, (*dikaion*.)" " There are two species of slavery, one founded in nature, the other in law. In the first, the master as fit to command as the slave to obey, their interests are mutual; and this community of interests begets good-will." By the " community of interests " he means that it is equally for the good of the slave as of the master, that the latter should command and control, as the former obey. " The master has a *right* to command." And it must be conceded, he further says, " that the slave is capable of virtues," is not a *mere tool*.

THE CHRISTIAN RELATION IN SLAVERY

" CAN there be a true Christian relation," asks Professor Lewis, in his last article, " between a man owned, and another man, who claims to be his owner?" We hesitate not to answer, *Yes:* especially as it is too evident to be controverted, that our blessed Lord, Paul and Peter, have answered it in the affirmative. You have only to read Christ's interview with the centurion, portions of Paul to the Corinthians, Ephesians, Colossians, to Timothy and Philemon, and of Peter's epistle, in order to feel it, as well as to see it. "The wayfaring man, though a fool, cannot err therein," and "he who runneth may read it." But the Professor answers his own question negatively, by attaching to the term *owning* the very acmé of "the *degradation* of humanity, its deepest *hurt*, its irreconcilableness with the oneness of believers in Christ, its debasement of the Christian life, and the Christian love, its low, repulsive, mercenary, earthly feeling." Now, all this, as it seems to us, is as much to be proven, as that *ownership* negates the Christian relation. In other words, it is begging the question, by a round-about way of piling up huge and monstrous epithets on that poor little pedestal of three letters, *own*. To bear so much, it should, at least, have been always written in capitals, OWN.

The distinction here made between the hired laborer and the slave, that the former has a "free will" and "room for all the moral relations," which the latter has not, is a distinction without a difference, a mere verbal logomachy. The free will, the absolute expressed choice or consent, is not essential to obligation on the one part, and right on the other. The rights and duties of parent and child depend on no *freedom of will*, no exercise of choice on the part of the child, but grow out of a natural and constituted relation between the parties, originating obligations. The same is true of the rights of government and the duties of subjects, specially whilst yet minors. Yet in these and other cases, there is full play-room for the moral relations, as much as in the case of the pinched and poorly-paid hired servant. And so of the slave. He, in the relation he bears to his master, under law, has room for all the moral relations, and has as much *free will* for the discharge of duty and the exercise of right as is either beneficial or desirable. Free will must be put under restraint of some kind or it runs, much more naturally and forcefully, into evil than to good. So did it with our mother Eve and our father Adam, and so has it done ever since when left unbridled and licensed. Give it the reins and it drives humanity, Jehu-like, to ruin. All law is restriction on free will; all government also, whether paternal, monarchical, tyrannical or republican; and one of the first injunctions of Christianity is, obedience even to self-constituted and hereditary Powers. Besides, it is a miserable *free* will, which chooses, under a *necessity*, to be harnessed, in nudity (woman too !) to the little car in the dark, deep mines !

The Professor next undertakes to show that the golden rule of the gospel can have no application in the relations of slavery, whilst in those of the hired service it has " perfect application." And his assertion is based on the fact, that it contains " a *would* and a *should*, a desire and a condition." " Whatsoever ye would that men should do : " " a mutual claim and a mutual *right*," which " cannot exist between an *owner* and what is owned." " There is here no *would and should*, no mutual *ought* involving a mutual *right*, and furnishing the ground of a mutual *love*." " The fact that the golden rule of love and obligation *can have no place* in this claim of servile ownership, shows that it lies out of the pale of Christianity."

These quotations give the full view of the Professor on this point, and, although perhaps taking and antithetic, we do not appreciate them as argumentative or forceful. We concede that, in the Savior's golden rule, for which the world must ever bless Him, there is a *would and a should*, the one expressing *condition* and *obligation*, the other *desire :* but we do not, in this concession, accept his conclusions. According to his own analysis of the rule, the desire or wish of the one party, we think, must be limited to that which is *right*, that which the other party *ought* to do. It cannot, of course, embrace every wanton or fanciful *would* or wish, but only such as you can rightfully feel, and the other would be bound, *obligated* to do. Your *would* must consist with his *should*. If men *should* do what you *would* they should, then you must do even so to them. Your *obligation* to do for others is not as extensive as might be your own wishes from others, but is relieved and regulated by the *rectitude* of your desires in regard to others. You must have a *right*, on principles of moral obligation, to demand of another, in the same circumstances, what you are bound to do for another. Now, the Professor asserts that things cannot exist, where there is property in man, that slavery destroys free will, mutuality of claim, of right, of love. He may, indeed, first convert a slave into an ass, a man into a brute, then thrust his convert down our throats, insist on his conception of slavery or ownership, and then deny to such *brute* all moral powers, all sense of right and wrong, and then jump very easily to the conclusion, that between him and an owning master there can be no mutual *ought*, no *mutual* right nor love ; and consequently, that " the golden rule," which implies responsible agents, " can have no place in this claim of servile ownership." This is not only fallacious reasoning, but it is equally in opposition to the action of the author of the rule. Did not Christ intend this golden maxim to apply to the relations he found existing in the Roman empire and in the families of his own followers? The question answers itself.

Now suppose we reverse the process, and reason thus. Christ proclaimed this law of love and his Apostles carried it out in exhortations and precepts, just when and where there existed, in and out of the church, an *ownership-slavery*, worse in many features than that of our Southern States. But there is in this law of love, the golden rule, " a *would* and a *should*," " an *ought* including a *will* and an *obligation :* there is a mutual claim and a mutual right." Then we are in a dilemma. Either Christ uttered his great law of social and Christian life knowing that it had " no application " to pervading relations of social life, or he announced it believing that, with its *would and should*, its *obligation and right*, it had just as much application to these relations of " servile ownership," as to any other. We accept the latter, and deduce the conclusion, that " the golden rule of love and obligation *can* have place" here ; that slavery does *not* " lie out of the pale of Christianity, out of the kingdom of God," but in it ; and that there is *not* in it " a dead absorption of every moral idea."

And then to talk as if in it there were " no ground of a mutual *love !* " Why the facts of the case are so opposite to this, as to offer the most triumphant overthrow of the statements which culminate in such a deduction. Where, in any other system of mutual dependence, any other system of service, not excepting the most gentle species of *hired* service ever extant, do you find such manifestations of mutual love? The very terms of address on both parts, the devotion of the slave to his master, his master's wife and children, and the tender returns of care and kindness on their part, have become proverbial, and cannot and do not exist where the *free hired service* prevails. If there is "no ground for this mutual love," this is a rare specimen of humanity, and we should be inclined to start a theory, not of *semi-homo*, semi-manhood, but of *super*-homo. But we abstain here from theories, intending to look at simple biblical facts.

The Professor avers, very consistently we grant, that "the hirer has a moral claim, because a free will has promised it;" but, in the other case, there can be no moral claim, because no free will, no voluntary contract. Then, fathers and mothers, beware that you do not too early listen to the Apostle's advice and exact obedience of your children. Beware, too, of the wisdom of Solomon, in this regard! Conscripts under the "dignity of power," rebel, desert your standards, rush into anarchy. There is "no moral claim," because "no *free will* of yours has promised the service!"

PROPERTY IN MAN. (LEWIS AND HODGE.)

In article seventh, Professor Lewis reverts to the old idea of property in man, or ownership, on which he had already dwelt at such length, in his primary articles. Now, mainly for the purpose of controverting and converting Dr. Hodge of Princeton, known and read of all men. In the latter hope, we presume, he is doomed to fail, as in the former, we think him utterly unsuccessful. The definition of Dr. Hodge is that "when one man is called the property of another, it can only mean that the one has the right *to use the services of another.*" This Dr. Lewis disputes, and pronounces a "sophism," substituting his own definition as the indisputable truth, to wit: "*Property in anything is simply property in the use or uses that may be made of that thing.*" "To complete the idea, there must be nothing in the thing owned, which, as will, can oppose the will of the owner in the free use of it ; nor any thing from without, which hinders its vendibility." "No room left for the distinction between ownership of a man, and that of a horse." "The one is a *right* to get all the uses possible out of a man ; the other, to get all the possible uses out of an animal." "The owner of a man has a right to the use of his will and of his Christianity."

What Dr. Hodge will say to all this we know not, but for ourselves we have to say, that there seems in it more of "*sophism*" than in the accepted definition of the Doctor. Very much of property is made so, becomes so, only by law, and the law may distinctly define the attributes of the property, we think, or leave them to be inferred from the nature of the case, the qualities and capacities of the thing owned. If the law, then, make a *man* property, it is competent, also, to define the nature of the property, and to restrict it to the *services of the man*, excluding the right to own his Christianity and his will. Or it can leave that to be determined by the nature and relations of the property. In this case man could not, by common consent nor common sense, become nor be considered property in the same sense with a horse or an ox or a farm. It is "Christianly and humanly inconceivable," to use one of the Professor's phrases.

But to the Professor's own definition. Wherein does it differ, really, from Dr. Hodge's ? The one is "right to *services ;* " the other "property in the *uses* to be made of a thing," or, as it should be, *right* to these uses. And, in fact, he himself considers them synonyms, immediately interpreting his definition thus : "Property in a horse is the right to *use* the animal as a horse, for the *service* a horse can do." There is sophism, here, in the Professor's use of the little word *may* in his definition quoted above, as he thinks there is in Dr. Hodge's use of *only* in his definition. He surely would not contend that property implies right to all *possible* uses of the thing owned. If not, to what uses, then, in case of a man, other than those implied, included in *services ?* Will he say that property, *proprium*, of necessity gives right to use a horse so as to abuse him, to violate his nature, to put him to uses not conformable to his being, however *possible* they might be? Much less can he rationally contend that property in man, intelligent man, necessarily gives right to use him as if he were not more than a brute, not possessed of a soul. Thus, whether you regard this property as founded in nature or constituted by law, you must limit your ideas of the property by the qualities of the object. Because you *own* the soil and may therefore plough it, it does not follow that you may plough the back of the slave, because you own him. If you own a bull, and may therefore chain him to his stall or use him purposely for the generation of his kind, it does not follow, from your owning a man, that you have a right to do the same things with him. There is no pretence, nor could there be any, that property in man includes the ownership of his soul, as the Professor contends. It is just ridiculous, and grows not out of any just definition of property ever before given; and we think neither the philosophic nor legal world will accept his own. It will probably remain his property, no one wishing ever to buy it, much less to claim it.

We do not confound " hired labor " with slave labor, and reason from one to the other, as some do. It is often more bitter, and is an abject slavery, yet is it not exactly compulsory. The man may choose to die rather than submit to it, but he is free, in a sense, to accept or reject the terms. Yet is this conceded distinction no proof that the one is right, the other wrong. Liberty to do as you choose, freedom from subjection to another, is not a necessity of manhood, nor always its *right*. We know it is said : " Man has a right to liberty." What right? Where did he get it? A right by his own nature? Doubted. A right given him of God, his Maker? Where? Let us not so hastily give ourselves up to dogmas, which may have no foundation in Scripture, but much in infidelity, and mere anthropology.

And now, on " the *practical* questions, as they would style them," he quotes from a sermon by Rev. Neal Cleavland, which we have not seen, as stating those questions well. " Does this relation contradict the laws of love ? " " Does it hinder a de-

sire after the spiritual and temporal welfare of servants?"
"What hinders to teach them the truths of the Gospel?" And
Professor Lewis answers this by simply remarking that pages
of just such questions could be asked, and adding: "Why,
nothing hinders, if you treat the man as your dependent and
benefactor," as Mr. C. had described the slave. "But this hinders, this claim of ownership, which is of the essence of modern slavery." "When it becomes supreme, it utterly extin-
guishes all Christian love." "Ownership is essential worldliness; there can be no deeper worldliness." "There is *no other*
ownership than to own for worldly gain." Remember, *ownership alone is the evil*, in the Professor's view. Not so thought
Christ and apostles. Yet the Professor pronounces Mr. C.
right in calling the slave the "benefactor" of his master.
If so, then, according to Aristotle, he is capable of the *higher
friendship*.

The fallacy and fault of the Professor's statements are
transparent, and seem to become translucent at least to himself. For he immediately devotes a large part of a column in
telling us, (after having settled and sealed it that ownership
is the essence, the virus of slavery,) that, "if the idea of ownership is discarded, except as under law, then we have no quarrel with them." Then there is no quarrel with a *legalized
ownership*, a slavery which rests on *law*, and discards extraneous evils. This is a frank surrender of his stronghold,
his Fort Sumter. After a terrible struggle, he at last evacu-
ates. He gives up the gist, and the half in length, of his
whole argument, that ownership, property in man, is the damning idea in slavery. This is very much like Lewis *versus*
Lewis, even in the same treatise.

But still, he rises again from his suicidal fall, and springs
upon the old game. Such an idea of slavery, he contends,
does not exist, and cannot exist. It is essentially mercenary,
low, selfish; and to prove it, he quotes again from a sermon
of "the Rev. James Smylie, of Amity Presbytery," who contends that buying, selling, holding a slave for gain, is not sin.
And, as if this doctrine were to be maintained on the basis of
the golden rule, or, at least, as consistent with it, he once more

reverts to this law of love, and gives us, definitively, his interpretation of it, and pronounces it an emphatic " precept against
slavery." His interpretation is : " Whatsoever ye may *rightly*
wish that men should do, etc. ; " and he thinks " there is implied
in it an unchanging equality, that exists among all true human
relations," and asserts, as conformable to this, that " all men
have an equal right to life and liberty." In this he differs
again from the " Pure Intellect," the great Stagyrite.

But it is apparent to every reflecting mind, that the question is only shoved a step further back : What may one *rightly*
wish ? May the slave rightly wish his liberty ? Aristotle
would answer, *No.* We, however, accept the Bible, and not
Aristotle, as our guide in this matter ; and although the Professor, by the ruling he so often applies to Mr. Van Dyke,
might be held to the literal precept, we are ready to grant the
essential rectitude of his rendering, agreeing as it does, with
that of Chalmers, and others of the best commentators. Then,
of course, it is to be determined whether or not the slave may
rightly, or whether or not he ought to, desire his liberty. This
necessarily opens up again the whole subject for discussion,
and the answer, if right, must be founded on the Word of
God. It seems, also to us, a pertinent question : Does it follow
that, because one party, in a certain relation to another, has
abstractly, or in some sense, a *right* to wish a thing, the other
party is bound to grant it ? A child might, in some sense,
rightly wish for something, and yet the parent not be bound,
all things considered, to grant it. A criminal, a prisoner might,
in certain regards, rightly wish exemption from chains, and
yet it might not be the duty of the State, *all things considered*,
to grant the wish. In both these cases, as in others, the wish
might be *right*, in view only of the nature, the sensibilities and
affections of the child or criminal, yet, in view of other consid-
erations, wider and higher, the duty to grant the wish would
not follow.

But, finally, to assure himself and others, that a Christian
man cannot hold a fellow-man, much less a fellow-Christian, as
property, he inquires : Who is the Christian man ? We accept
every word of his Scriptural answer to this question. He is

"a pilgrim," "a seeker of a better country," "a sojourner," "seeking a city which hath foundations," "one who felt that the fashion of the world was passing away," "who sought not his own," "whose citizenship was in heaven," "looking for a crown of glory," one who "loved others as he loved himself, even better," "a friend of Christ," "a brother beloved," "one who regards the poor, and gives him a high place, higher than the rich." And we add, one whose "affection was set on things above, and not on things on the earth," who felt that, "though the outward man perish, the inward is renewed day by day; for the light affliction, which is but for a moment, worketh out a far more exceeding and eternal weight of glory, whilst we look not at the things seen, but at the things not seen; for the things seen are *temporal*, but the things not seen, *eternal*."

This is just that "interior spirit" of the entire Bible, of which we have already spoken, and which made it of small account to Christ or his apostles to dwell on the mere temporal relations of life; of little moment to the slave to pant after a legal, political liberty, if so be he were the freedman of Christ; which led Paul to tell him, if he became a Christian, being a slave, not to care much for *that*, but to abide patiently and Christianly in his calling, and which authorized the master to say: "Let the dead bury their dead:" there are higher interests than those even of the tenderest family relations.

We may, in other issues, take up some related subjects, and should like much, even in this, to draw a comparison between the exercises of governmental and of slave power; but as our sole object now is to reply to the articles of Professor Lewis as briefly as possible, we abstain from further discussion and enlargement, and leave what we have written in the hands of Him who is the source of all truth, that He may give it its proper effect. If there is error, our prayer is that we may see it; if truth, that we and others may be established in it.

THE END.

www.ingramcontent.com/pod-product-compliance
Lightning Source LLC
Chambersburg PA
CBHW021529090426
42739CB00007B/856

* 9 7 8 3 7 4 4 7 3 1 3 4 8 *